Picture the Past

DERBY

ACKNOWLEDGEMENTS

Several people have assisted me in my research for this book and I would particularly like to thank the following for their help and support: Ron Adamson, Derby Heritage Forum, Joan Darcy, Gillian Eardley, Mark Higginson, John Hollinshead and John Plant.

Picture the Past

DERBY

Denis Eardley

www.picturethepast.org.uk

First published in Great Britain in 2012 by The Derby Books Publishing Company Limited, 3 The Parker Centre, Derby, DE21 4SZ.

ISBN 978-1-85983-829-7
Printed and bound by Gomer.

CONTENTS

INTRODUCTION

In the past, anyone wanting to view the collections of hundreds of thousands of old images in the libraries and museums of Derbyshire or Nottinghamshire would have had to travel many miles to try and track down the ones they were interested in. This proved to be frustrating and time consuming for researchers, a barrier to anyone from further afield and damaging to the more fragile images from all the handling. The collections include photographs, slides, negatives, glass plates, postcards and engravings recalling the history of our local communities for a hundred years and more.

Thankfully senior staff from the local authorities of Derbyshire and Nottinghamshire County Councils and the City Councils of Derby and Nottingham, combined ideas to solve the problem and the concept of conserving the images using digitisation, while at the same time giving people all over the world access to the digitised versions, was conceived.

In 2002 funding was obtained from the Heritage Lottery Fund and, together with additional money from the four partner authorities, the project was established in offices above Heanor Library with Nick Tomlinson managing a team of experienced professionals inputting the information to a custom-built database and carefully digitising the images. In 2012 the project office was moved to Derbyshire Record Office in Matlock, as part of a plan to bring the local studies libraries and archives together under one roof.

Local studies staff out in the libraries and museums collate images and information ready for inclusion in the project and sort out obtaining copyright clearance from the owners of the original photographs before sending them up to the project office for scanning.

The Picture the Past website (www.picturethepast.org.uk) was launched in June 2003 and in 2012 the project celebrated adding the 100,000th picture.

Regularly attracting well over 10,000 visitors a month, from all over the world, viewing hundreds of thousands of pages of images, the site has been designed to be as 'easy to use' as possible. With a simple keyword search facility, as well as more comprehensive search tools, it gives the user the ability to easily find images relating to their town or village and actually encourages them to 'add-to' or 'correct' existing information.

The site is updated on a regular basis and visitors can print out low-resolution copies directly from the site for their own personal use or study purposes for free. For those users wanting to own a top-quality copy for themselves, the website includes an online ordering service with the option to buy their favourite images printed on a range of items including glass chopping boards, coasters, mouse mats, cards as well as more traditional prints to hang on their walls (see below). As a non-profit making project, all the income raised from this service goes back into the conservation and preservation of more original pictures.

This book draws heavily on the 'Picture the Past' resources and gives you the chance to sample just a handful of the images contained on the website and it is very much hoped that you will go on to enjoy the rest of the pictures online.

For people who do not have access to the Internet at home, or who are not sure where to start, there are computers available for public use in all libraries and the local studies staff are more than willing to help you get started.

Picture the Past can be contacted at: Derbyshire County Council, Derbyshire Record Office, County Hall, Matlock DE4 3AG. Tel: +44 (0)1629 533809. Fax: +44 (0)1629 57611

The website is completely free to use and can be accessed at

www.picturethepast.org.uk

Examples of some of the products we offer.

The 'Picture the Past' team won an award in the 2007 Local Government IT Excellence Awards. The awards highlight the use of best practice in local government and how IT has been used both effectively and innovatively to deliver best-value public services. The judges commended the project team's commitment to utilise technology in order to preserve the region's heritage.

In 2004, the website also won the Alan Ball Local History Award in recognition of its commitment to local history publishing.

CHAPTER I - THE RAILWAY QUARTER

In the 1830s Derby was struggling to attract sufficient trade and as a result a public meeting was held at the Town Hall in December 1835. It was decided that the lack of a good communication system, where goods could be moved quickly and inexpensively, was the main problem. Voting was unanimous to support petitions to be put before Parliament to bring the railways to Derby, and the following year Parliament passed an act allowing the existing railway network to be linked to the town.

Three railway companies were involved in running lines into Derby, the Midland Counties, the North Midland Railway Company, and the Birmingham and Derby Junction Railway Company. They decided that sharing a station would be the most inexpensive solution and, after considerable debate, a site was selected. It lay one mile to the south of the town, with only about one third situated within the Borough, the remainder being in the small township of Litchurch.

On the 30 May 1839 at 1.18pm, the first railway train steamed into Derby stopping at a temporary wooden platform a little to the south of the present station. The engine, named 'Sunbeam' had completed the journey from Nottingham in 48 minutes, pulling four first class and two second class carriages. A second train, 'Ariel', arrived one minute later, having covered the journey from Nottingham in 44 minutes. It later returned to its starting point, before returning to Derby in 31 minutes at an average speed of 30mph.

Five days later, the Midland Counties Railway Company started a regular passenger service between Derby and Nottingham. This was soon followed by the Birmingham and Derby Junction Railway, who began a regular service between the two locations, shortly after the opening ceremony on 5 August. It was the 30 June, in the following year, before the North Midland line was opened to Leeds, a journey of 72 miles.

The three independent companies joined together on the 10 May 1844 to form the Midland Railway Company, as swarms of workers began to flock to Derby. They came from all parts of the country and by 1851 records showed that 43% of the adults in the town had been born outside the county. The majority were employed in the railway works, where Locomotive, Carriage and Wagon, Signal and Telegraph works were established. Others were employed by companies that had been formed because of the railway's arrival, as well as existing companies that were able to expand for the same reason.

Trail: Derby Midland Railway Station – Midland Road – London Road (detour south) – London Road (north) – return to Railway Terrace – Midland Place (detour) – Railway Terrace - Siddals Road – Pride Park – return to Derby Midland Railway Station.

Railway Bridge over the River Derwent. *This view of the Five Arches railway bridge dates back to the time the bridge was constructed in 1839. It crossed the River Derwent to the north of the station and was paid for by the North Midland Railway, and still remains in use today. The girder bridge over the former Derby Canal, paid for by the Midland Counties Railway, is now dominated by the modern road viaduct carrying Pride Parkway over the railway. In the foreground a group of people are haymaking. Farming at that time was largely labour intensive with only hand tools and a horse and cart to help.*

DMAG001987 - Picture courtesy of Derby Museums and Art Gallery

DCHQ200344 - Picture courtesy of Miss Frances Webb

Derby Railway Station, 19th century. *A lithograph showing the interior of Derby Station, shortly after construction had been completed in 1840. The three-bay train sheds take up the centre of the picture, with the Midlands Counties Railway's platform on the right and the locomotive workshops of the North Midlands Railway are on the left. On the extreme left is the engine shed of the Midland Counties Railway. A railway policeman is seen on the right, using hand signals to assist the driver of the locomotive in a shunting operation. Cut throat competition between the three railway companies, led to a lack of co-operation in the sharing of the station and uneconomic pricing structures. The problem was solved in 1844 with the amalgamation of the three railway companies, forming the Midland Railway.*

Aerial view of Derby Midland Railway Station. *This is the oldest known photograph taken of Derby Railway Station and is thought to date back to about 1860. It has been taken from the roof of the station and shows the Locomotive and Carriage Works in the foreground. The Midland Railway was formed on the 10 May 1844, by the amalgamation of three companies who had originally shared the station. The station was further enlarged in 1867 and 1881. It was demolished in 1985 and replaced with the current modern station. The Coat of Arms of both the Midland Railway and the City of Derby enhance the station frontage. The original station clock has been re-sited at the top end of the Railway Terrace Car Park.*

DRBY005939 - Picture courtesy of Derby City Council

DMAG300086 - Picture courtesy of Derby Museums and Art Gallery

Railway shed at Derby Station. *Work on Derby Railway Station did not start until the autumn of 1839, and temporary arrangements were made for the intervening period between the commencement of railway services and the completion of the station. It was built by Thomas Jackson and designed by Francis Thompson and paid for by the North Midland Railway, the other two railway companies who also operated from the site being charged rent. It was completed during the summer of 1840. The extremely long platform of 1,050 feet, originally thought by some to be too large for requirements soon became very busy. The platforms were rebuilt in the early 1950s following war damage.*

Aerial view of Derby Railway Station and Railway works. *The Midland Railway Company acquired a small site in Derby in the 1840s and built workshops to repair their rail vehicles. This site soon expanded and in 1876 a further site was acquired, which became the Carriage and Wagon Works. The original site was then devoted to the building and repair of locomotives. The picture was taken on the 11 November 1978, looking North West at the Railway Station and Railway works, with the Roundhouse, centre right. Built in 1844, after the formation of the Midland Railway Company, the Roundhouse was used for the repair of the companies steam trains.*

DRBY003072 - Picture courtesy of Derby Evening Telegraph

DMAG000244 - Picture courtesy of Derby Museums and Art Gallery

Derby Railway Station at night. *This pre 1904 picture is one of Valentine's Moonlight Series and shows an attractive moonlit view of the frontage of the Midland Railway Station. The Town Council wanted the station sited close to the town centre, but the railway companies mindful of the extra expense wanted it further away. Several alternative sites for the station were considered, but no decision was taken until after the formation of a committee representing both Derby Town Council and the railway companies. Eventually a site at the Old Meadows was selected, the council agreeing to improve the approaches and the railway companies to build a bridge over the Derby Canal and River Derwent. Once full agreement had been reached, planning permission was granted and work on the station started.*

Derby Railway Station frontage. *An electric tram and horse-drawn cabs are seen in this c1908 picture outside Derby Railway Station. The station slowly deteriorated over the years and although improvements and repairs were undertaken periodically, the main station buildings were urgently in need of costly repairs, so the decision to demolish was taken. Plans for a new modern station were drawn up and work began in December 1985. In order to retain a connection with the old station, the Coat of Arms of the Midland Railway and also the City of Derby are displayed on the front of the station with the former station clock set on a plinth at the end of the car park.*

DRBY004354 - Picture courtesy of Derby City Council

DMAG001117 - Picture courtesy of Derby Museums and Art Gallery

Derby Electricity Department Outing. *This is a picture of a group of the County Borough of Derby Electricity Department employees, in the 1920s outside Derby Midland Railway Station. They are presumably just about to set off on a departmental outing. Derby became a centre for day excursions, the railway companies encouraging people to travel and discover new places and revisit former destinations. Thomas Cook who was born in a small cottage in Quick Close, Melbourne in 1808, became known throughout the world for the travel company he founded. At the age of 28, he moved to Leicester to work for the Baptist Church. His first organised trip was to transport, by rail, passengers from Leicester to Loughborough and back again. The 570 passengers attended a temperance rally at the cost of one shilling each. This was successful, as were other trips and the railway company asked him to organise excursions. Cook used Derby as one of the picking up points. His business continued to expand rapidly taking in other forms of transportation and other countries.*

The relief of Mafeking. *Crowds gathered outside the Midland Railway Station following the relief of Mafeking during the Boer War. The Midland Hotel in the background was built to a high standard to meet the requirements of travellers, by Thomas Jackson, the Pimlico builder, to the design of Francis Thompson, the Midland Railway architect. It was the first purpose-built railway hotel in the country, and is still one of the finest hotels in the city. Many famous people, including Queen Victoria in 1849, have stayed at the hotel, which was intended for first class passengers. Originally, it was known as Cuff's Midland Hotel, Cuff also being the manager of the station refreshment rooms. In 1862, it was purchased by the railway company and became the Midland Hotel. It is now in private hands and has been renamed the Hallmark following a recent refurbishment.*

DMAG000243 - Picture courtesy of Derby Museums and Art Gallery

DRBY002617 - Picture courtesy of Derby City Council

Midland Road. *This picture has been taken on a busy day in 1904, looking down Midland Road towards the station, shortly after the introduction of Electric Trams. The premises on the right, with large church-like windows, were designed as a purpose built studio for William Walter Winter, the well respected local photographer. Winter had started business on the opposite side of the road in 1864, but three years later moved to his new home. The studio faced north to protect it as far as possible from direct sunlight. Following a fire in the 1880s, Winter carried out a reorganisation of the building, adding a new studio and artist's room. In 1921, a War Memorial designed by Sir Edwin Lutyens, who also designed the Cenotaph in London, was added near to the Midland Hotel.*

Crowds and troops await the arrival of King Edward VII, Midland Road. *A picture looking down Midland Road, which has been taken on the 28 June 1906, the occasion of King Edward VII's visit to Derby to unveil the statue of his mother, Queen Victoria, on The Spot. The Crown and Cushion, on the left hand corner of Midland Road, was built in 1853, no doubt with the intention of benefiting from the boom created by the arrival of the railway workers. The name is usually associated with the monarchy, when the crown is presented on a silk tasselled cushion at Coronations. Arthur Cecil Felix, the grandfather of Richard Felix, the former owner of Derby Heritage Centre, was the landlord during the Edwardian era.*

DRBY006640 - Picture courtesy of Derby City Council

DRBY004796 - Picture courtesy of Derby City Council

St Andrew's Church, London Road (south). *A short distance south along London Road is the place where St Andrew's Church used to stand, before it was demolished in 1970 and replaced by St Andrew's House. The church was always regarded as the Railwaymen's Church and dominated the skyline of London Road in this picture taken in the early 1900s. The Midland Railway contributed generously towards its building fund to ensure that the spiritual needs of its ever growing workforce were met. It was consecrated in 1866, but it took another 25 years before the spire was finally completed. Sir George Gilbert Scott, who designed London's St Pancras Station, was the designer.*

London Road (north). *A c1905, postcard view of London Road, which shows two well dressed ladies and a lady and gentleman in the foreground, all of whom appear to be taking a leisurely stroll in the sunshine along the tree-lined street. On the extreme left is the Congregational Church and to the right of it is Frank Porter's Removals business. London Road was turnpiked in 1738 to enable the journey to and from the capital to be improved. In 1840, Midland Road was built to link London Road to the Midland Railway Station. Electric trams were introduced in 1904.*

DRBY005105 - Picture courtesy of Derby City Council

DRBY004779 - Picture courtesy of Derby City Council

Derby Royal Infirmary, c1904 (Now London Road Hospital). *In 1806, leading residents of Derby opened a public subscription to build what was to be known as the Derby General Infirmary. William Strutt, a descendant of Jedediah the industrialist, incorporated many revolutionary designs into the new hospital. These included a hot air plant for heating and ventilation and many other labour saving devices and the hospital was considered one of the most advanced of its time. But it was discovered that the ventilation ducts could not be properly cleaned and were in fact causing disease. This led in the 1860s to an above average death rate and as no solution could be found, Florence Nightingale advised the hospital should be re-built. On the 21 May 1891, Queen Victoria came to Derby and laid the foundation stone for the new hospital. As a consequence it was granted a royal title as the Derbyshire Royal Infirmary.*

Derby Corporation Horse Trams, London Road. *A horse drawn tram in the early 1900s, making its way past the turn for Trinity Street. The London Road route was opened by the Derby Tramways Company from the Market Place to the Midland Station in 1880 and extended to Deadman's Lane the following year. It was largely single track with passing loops at intervals. Derby Corporation took over the Tramway Co. in 1899. The left-hand car appears to be number 22, one of a batch purchased secondhand by the new owners from Glasgow Corporation in 1901-3. The unidentified car on the right may be another example of the same type. The London Road route was converted to electric operation in 1904 and the horse trams ran for the last time in Derby in 1907.*

DMAG001407 - Picture courtesy of Derby Museums and Art Gallery

DRBY003211 - Picture courtesy of Derby City Council

Florence Nightingale statue, London Road. *The statue of Florence Nightingale is situated in the grounds of the former DRI, facing London Road. It was the measures she took to save the injured during the Crimean War that made her famous and, she became a legend in her own lifetime. Born in Italy on the 12 May 1820, she was named Florence after the city where she first drew breath. On returning to England, the Nightingales divided their time between two homes at Lea Hurst in Derbyshire and Embley in Hampshire. Social life did not satisfy Florence and to the family's dismay she expressed the desire to take up nursing. After many passionate arguments, she eventually got her way and despite the continuing opposition of her family, she took up an appointment as manager of the Institution for the Care of Sick Gentlewomen in Distressed Circumstances in London. It was not long after this that she went to the Crimea and became a legend - the Lady with the Lamp, whose shadow the sick soldiers kissed as she passed through the wards. On returning to England, Florence devoted the rest of her life to improving public health and providing proper training for nurses. At the age of 87, she was awarded the Order of Merit, the first woman ever to receive the award. However, she did not forget her connections with Lea Hurst setting up a reading room in Holloway and providing books there and to Lea Primary School. For the sick, she obtained the services of a doctor. She died in retirement in Buckinghamshire in 1910. The Duke of Devonshire unveiled Florence Nightingale's statue at the DRI, on the 12 June 1914. On the other side of London Road at 1 Trinity Street is the Nightingale Home. It is associated with the Royal Derby and Derbyshire Nursing Institution. The nursing home was also a training school for midwives and district nurses. It is now closed.*

DRBY004573 - Picture courtesy of Derby Evening Telegraph

Liversage Almshouses, London Road. *Further along London Road towards the city centre are the Liversage Trust Almshouses, built out of the Liversage estate. Robert Liversage, a master dyer and tradesman, had become very wealthy during the first half of the 16th century, but died a childless man in 1529. Together with his wife, they left all their land and property to the poor of St Peter's Parish, where they lived. This led to the establishment of the Liversage Charity Trust, the value of which increased enormously over the years. In 1836, Derby architect John Mason designed, along London Road, 21 almshouses with a chapel and hospital. The houses had a front room, small kitchen, pantry, one bedroom and lavatory with gardens at the rear and a lawn at the front. The occupants were provided with coal and a coat or cloak each year. All the occupants were given a shilling a week to live on, but only parishioners who had not received any other parish relief and were of the 'best moral character' were allowed to live in the houses.*

DMAG000366 - Picture courtesy of Derby Museums and Art Gallery

The former Railway Institute, Railway Terrace. *Ten years after the arrival of the railway, the Railway Institute was founded as a reading room for Midland Railway employees. It is an impressive red brick building, with its name spelt out in terracotta facing bricks, facing onto Railway Terrace. It opened on the 16th February 1894, as a cultural centre for railway workers. At one time it contained a library of 18,000 books, a concert hall with a stage and sitting for 500 people. In addition, there were several other rooms set on one side for dining, meetings and games. By the 1980s, the Railway Institute had been leased off to the Post Office Social Club, but that closed in 1994. Following the failure of plans to convert it into an arts centre, it was opened as a pub in 1996, called The Waterfall.*

DMAG000687 - Picture courtesy of Richard Keene Ltd

Bemrose Printers and Co, Midland Place, Off Railway Terrace. *This picture, taken around 1860, shows the premises on Midland Place of Bemrose and Sons the printers. The arrival of the railways led to the expansion of many existing Derby businesses. William Bemrose, who in 1840, for example, employed a staff of only twelve at his printing and stationery business in Derby Market Place, saw business increase dramatically. He was awarded the contract for Midland Railway time-tables and stationary and by 1855 the number of workers had increased to 57 and in 1871 to 228. The organization continued to grow into the huge Bemrose Corporation, which employed many thousands of workers. The road is being resurfaced in the picture and a timber yard with a crane can be seen in the background.*

Railway Terrace Cottages. *In order to accommodate the more senior Midland Railway staff, Jackson and Thompson built a triangular block of streets called North Street (now Calvert Street), Midland Place and Railway Terrace. The initial letter from the three streets, results in NMR, which stands for North Midland Railway. The two smaller squares, Leeds Place and Sheffield Place, continue the railway theme named after cities on the line. This was the first development of its kind in the country and when in 1970, it was decided to demolish it there was strong opposition to the plan. Derbyshire Historic Buildings Trust stepped in with a modernisation plan and the Council dropped their proposals.*

DRBY004560 - Picture courtesy of Derby Evening Telegraph

Brunswick, Railway Terrace. *This picture was taken in 1983, when the cottages and the Brunswick Inn, built for the use of railwaymen and second class passengers were in a very poor state of repair. Opened in 1842, it was originally called 'The Brunswick Railway and Commercial Inn' and remained in the ownership of the railways for 105 years. After a long period of inactivity, it was rescued from the threat of demolition, together with the other railway cottages following work undertaken on behalf of the Derby Civic Society and the Derbyshire Historic Buildings Trust. It re-opened in 1987 and was purchased by Trevor Harris, who established a brewery on the premises. Since then, the pub has won several awards for its beer.*

DRBY004601 - Picture courtesy of Derby Evening Telegraph

Alexandra Hotel, Siddals Road. *The Alexandra Hotel near the new Pride Park flyover is named after HRH Princess Alexandra, who married the future Edward VII on the 10 March 1863. It became the birthplace of Derby CAMRA in 1974, but despite this was closed for demolition in 1987. For two years it remained boarded up before being rescued by Bateman's Brewery. It is Derby's only Real Ale pub offering accommodation. The wall by the road between the Alexandra and the Brunswick Inn identifies where the former Derby Canal once ran. In 1841/2 Siddals Road was extended to connect with Railway Terrace to improve access to the railway Station.*

DRBY000323 - Picture courtesy of Derby Evening Telegraph

DRBY004433 - Picture courtesy of Derby Evening Telegraph

Locomotive Works, Roundhouse Road. *At first the repair and manufacturing facilities for the three companies was separate, but following the formation of the Midland Railway Company, in 1844, they were concentrated at Derby. Matthew Kirtley was appointed as Locomotive and Carriage & Wagon Superintendent for the new company and by September 1851, the first locomotive had been completed and four years later the number had risen to 33. The workshops continued to grow and by the 1860s employed over 2,000 men. In 1876 a further site was acquired, which became the Carriage & Wagon Works. The original site was devoted to the building and repair of locomotives, the last steam train leaving the works in 1957. In total 2,941 steam locomotives and 1,010 diesel locomotives were produced before closure near the end of the last century. The Locomotive Works Offices were eventually sold to Derby College as a campus and social centre and have recently been renovated.*

Derby Roundhouse, Roundhouse Road. *The Roundhouse site with its storage sheds and historic locomotive turntable had been deteriorating, since it was for the most part vacated in 1990. The city council took over the site in 1994, when only the offices under the clock tower were occupied and the rest of the site was in a dilapidated state. This was recognised by English Heritage, who listed it the same year, along with the complex of listed buildings, in their Buildings at Risk Register. After several plans to save it had failed, this historic site is once again something that all Derby people can look on with great pride, following Derby College's superb restoration.*

DRBY003495 - Picture courtesy of Eric Matthews

The Queen and the Duke of Edinburgh at Pride Park Football Ground. *'Derbyshire Celebrates' was a Derbyshire flavoured pageant that took place on the 1 August 2002, in the presence of HM Queen and the Duke of Edinburgh to celebrate her Golden Jubilee. In 1993 plans were drawn up for Derby County to move to Pride Park, but this did not come about as originally planned. The football club decided to remain, where it was and redevelop the Baseball Ground. However, in a dramatic move, with work scheduled to start within a few days, the club had second thoughts and reopened talks about moving to Pride Park. Derby County Football Club's impressive stadium aptly, named Pride Park, now forms the centrepiece of the development. The stadium was opened by HM the Queen, on 18th July, 1997. Unfortunately, the first league match at the stadium, against Wimbledon FC, ended in embarrassment when the match had to be abandoned due to floodlight failure. Representative football came to Pride Park for the first time in February 1999 when England under 21s played the French under 21 team. This was followed in May 2001 by a full-international mach, England versus Mexico, played in front of what was, at the time, a record crowd for the stadium.*

The Sanctuary, Pride Park. *At the rear of the Park-and-Ride Car Park on Pride Park is 'The Sanctuary' a bird and wildlife reserve. It was formerly a gas works tip, and had long been protected from development as part of the 'green wedge' policy of Derby City Council. However, it was not until 2001 that the importance and potential of this site was fully appreciated, when the work to create the Pride Park business site came to a close. The site has deliberately been kept quite bare and devoid of trees, which attracts birds like the skylark, meadow pipit, the common tern and many other species. Access is not possible onto The Sanctuary itself, without special permission. All main features can be easily viewed from a number of points around the perimeter fencing, all accessible from the car park. At the time of writing, it is open Monday-Saturday 7am to 7pm, but closed on Sundays and home football match days.*

CHAPTER 2 - ST PETER'S QUARTER

The Lanes (now part of St Peter's Quarter) referred to as 'Derby's Hidden Gems' is bounded by Green Lane, Babington Lane, St Peter's Churchyard and Gower Street. They feature a wide range of interesting buildings, illustrating architectural trends from the mid-19th century to the 1960s. Most talked about today is probably the Hippodrome on Green Lane, which having been acquired by a developer entered 2012 in a state of near collapse. Designed in 1913, by Derby architect Alexander McPherson, this once popular Music Hall has been used in recent years as a Bingo Hall, before the owners decided to sell up and move to new premises.

After serving its time as a Music Hall, it was used as a cinema, before being acquired by Prince Littler, when The Grand Theatre closed in 1950. It had previously written its name into the theatrical history books, when the first performance of the adaption of Bram Stoker's famous vampire novel, Count Dracula, went on stage. The play later became a big hit on the London stage.

The tradition for Shrovetide Football started in the 18th century and in Derby all able bodied men living south of Markeaton Brook were named after the parish of 'St. Peter's', and those living north of it were called 'All Saints'. Proceedings commenced outside the Guildhall, when the ball was 'Turned up' on Shrove Tuesday each year and finished on Ash Wednesday. Shops and businesses were boarded up as the whole town was the pitch including the river and the brook. The objective was to score a goal either at Nun's Mill or at an agreed point on Osmaston Road. The game was so brutal that a number of attempts to stop it were made, before it was finally abolished. A French prisoner of war once said about the game, 'If the English call this playing, it would be impossible to say what they call fighting.'

Mary Queen of Scots was detained in Derby in 1569 and guarded by Sir Ralph Sadler. She stayed at Babington Hall, at a time when the house was let to Henry Beaumont whose wife acted as her hostess. Anthony Babington had acted as page to Mary and as a Roman Catholic supported her cause. In 1586, he was persuaded to take a leading role in a plot to assassinate Queen Elizabeth and place Mary on the throne. Babington Hall was sold to raise funds for the ultimately unsuccessful plot, which led to both his and Mary's execution.

Derby Grammar School is believed to be the second oldest grammar school in the country. It has had many famous pupils, including: Rev. John Cotton, Pilgrim Father who became a leading light in the church of New England, John Flamsteed, the first Astronomer Royal who founded the Greenwich Observatory and Joseph Wright, the internationally famous artist. The school received a Royal Charter and endowments from Queen Mary in 1544 and remained on the site next door to St. Peter's Church until moving to St. Helen's House in the 1860s.

Trail: Green Lane – Degge Street off Green Lane – Babington Lane – The Spot – St Peter's Street – (detour) St Peter's Churchyard Street – St Peter's Street.

DMAG300098 - Picture courtesy of Derby Museums and Art Gallery

Green Lane *A delightful 1926 picture painted by the landscape painter, Harold Gresley, looking down Green Lane from the corner of Wilson Street to Victoria Street, with trees on either side and good quality buildings lining the route. The spire of All Saints Church can be clearly seen in the distance. It became the Cathedral Church of All Saints in 1927. Harold Gresley was born in 1892 and lived all his life in Chellaston, along with his brother Cuthbert, father Frank and grandfather James. After service in the First World War, he studied at Nottingham School of Art and during 1925-26, he produced a series of Derby townscapes that later became part of the Goodey Collection. He also produced many paintings of Derbyshire beauty spots and country houses.*

DRBY005297 - Picture courtesy of Derby City Council

Aerial view looking from Green Lane towards the Corn Market and Victoria Street. *An aerial photograph, which was taken in 1935, shows the street layout from the Green Lane intersection with St Peter's Churchyard to St James' Street and the Market Place. Green Lane was originally called Green Hill. It runs from Brookside, now known as Victoria Street, to Normanton Road, where it turns south-west. In the early part of the 19th century, much of the land to the west side of the street was owned by the Rev Roseingrave Macklin, who gave his name to Macklin Street. The Forman family of Abbott's Hill House owned most of the land to the east.*

DMAG200524 - Picture courtesy of Derby Museums and Art Gallery

Mile Post, Green Lane. *The cast iron milepost, in the style of John Harrison's Bridge Street foundry is on the opposite side of Green Lane to the Hippodrome. It is inscribed 'Burton 11 miles'. Green Lane was originally the main road between Burton and Derby until Abbey Street was constructed in the 1820s. The buildings that line the street are mainly late Regency and early Victorian and range from workers' cottages to more palatial villas. At the bottom end of Green Lane the properties have been mostly converted into shops, with living accommodation and businesses further along.*

DCHQ502928 - Picture courtesy of A P Knighton

Hippodrome, Green Lane. *Designed in 1913, by Derby architect Alexander MacPherson, the Hippodrome, was built on the site of Green Hill House. This had been Derby's first private lunatic asylum. After it was superseded by the County Asylum at Mickleover in 1849, it was divided into two villas. It was eventually demolished to provide the site for the new theatre, which opened in 1914, with an audience capacity of 2,300. Between 1930 and 1950 it was also used as a cinema with the seating capacity reduced to 1,800. However, it became a theatre again in 1950, when J Arthur Rank agreed to sell the venue to Prince Littler, but on Monday 19 January 1959, the headline in the Derby Evening Telegraph carried the news:'Hippodrome closing not likely to re-open'. During its life, it had played host to stars such as Maria Lloyd, Flanagan and Allen, George Formby and, in later years, Morecambe and Wise, Ken Dodd and Tommy Cooper.*

DRBY007866 - Picture courtesy of Derby City Council

Hippodrome following acquisition by Mecca. *The Hippodrome having made a loss for the last three years running closed in 1959 and the premises were placed on the market. They were acquired by the entertainment company Mecca who re-opened it as a Bingo Hall and Social Club on 25 April 1962. The Hippodrome finally closed in 2007, and was sold for £375,000 to a private developer and at the time of writing is in a state of near collapse. Originally, the Hippodrome opened in 1914 as a music hall and palace of varieties and later became a cinema. It was the pending closure of the Grand that made the Hippodrome a target for Prince Littler, who agreed a deal with Rank. The Grand closed on the 9 December 1950 and the Hippodrome opened on the 23rd of the same month, after the transfer of the stage equipment.*

DRBY002030 - Picture courtesy of Derby City Council

'Boden's House' or 'Abbott's Hill House' Degge Street. *Degge Street, opposite Wilson Street was once the drive to Abbott's Hill House. The house was built c1720 for Sir Simon Degge. In 1789, the Improvement Commissioners had Babington Lane, built through the grounds of St Peter's (later Babington) House and Abbott's Hill House to join Green Lane. The house was in the hands of Colonel Walter Boden of 'The Pastures', Littleover, at the beginning of the 20th century. He owned a lace mill which operated in the vicinity. Boden died in 1905 and after that the property remained unoccupied for a time, before it was demolished in the mid-1920s.*

The Municipal Technical College, Green Lane. *A c1880 image of the former Technical College on Green Lane, a Grade II* listed building, built in Neo-Gothic style but with Arts and Crafts similarities. The building was designed by Thomas Simmonds, the new college's principal, in partnership with his friend and former fellow student, a Gloucester architect F.W.Waller, son-in-law of T H Huxley. It was completed in 1876 as the Municipal Technical College and enlarged in 1894. On 19 January 1899, the then Municipal Technical College for education in Science, Technology and Art was formally opened by the Duke of Devonshire, the President of the Board of Education. Since then students studying at Green Lane have been under the umbrella of various educational bodies including the Derby School of Art, Derby College of Art and the University of Derby. Designers, metalsmiths, architects, printers, painters and decorators and a wide variety of artists have studied there over the years prior to closure.*

DRBY003847 - Picture courtesy of Derby City Council

DRBY002512 - Picture courtesy of Derby Evening Telegraph

Metro Cinema, Green Lane. *The Metro Cinema opened for business on 15 January 1981, at the Derby Central School of Art, with a screening of the classic French comedy M. Hulot's Holiday, for an invited audience. This was followed by the first public screening of Derek Jarman's version of The Tempest. After six months the cinema was proving sufficiently popular to start a membership scheme. Originally it only opened on Thursdays, Fridays and Saturdays, but demand was so great that it started to open seven days a week. Shortly after celebrating its 25th anniversary, the cinema transferred to the University of Derby's Heap Lecture Theatre finally closing there during March 2008, prior to moving to the Quad, Derby's new £10m visual arts and media centre, on the 28 September 2008. The Metro was very much involved in the community, developing regional and city-wide initiatives, supporting local groups and organisations. It only had one screen, and 126 seats, but gave audiences the red velvet cinema experience. The picture was taken in 1989 outside the cinema.*

Victorian buildings on Green Lane. *Green Lane has been built up steadily over the years with a wide variety of Regency and Victorian houses. The three houses opposite the former Technical College, with their pointed gables, are of particular note and Grade II listed. They were built by Nottingham architect Thomas Chambers Hine in 1851-52 for Alderman Henry Darby. He, like Robert Forman, a rich maltster who owned much of the land to the east of Green Lane, eventually filled the role of mayor in the town. On the corner of Wilson Street and Green Lane, nearest the centre of Derby, is an 1862 villa, which has been impressively rebuilt by Derby architects Browning and Hayes in 1931-32 for the use of the Beaconsfield Conservative Club. The picture was taken in 1984.*

DMAG200525 - Picture courtesy of Derby Museums and Art Gallery

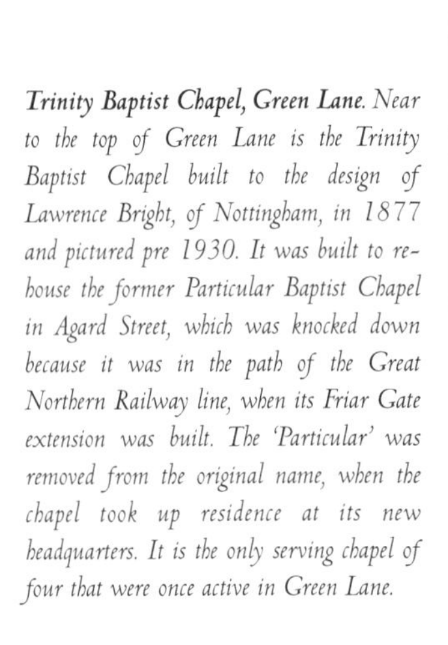

Trinity Baptist Chapel, Green Lane. *Near to the top of Green Lane is the Trinity Baptist Chapel built to the design of Lawrence Bright, of Nottingham, in 1877 and pictured pre 1930. It was built to re-house the former Particular Baptist Chapel in Agard Street, which was knocked down because it was in the path of the Great Northern Railway line, when its Friar Gate extension was built. The 'Particular' was removed from the original name, when the chapel took up residence at its new headquarters. It is the only serving chapel of four that were once active in Green Lane.*

DCHQ005629

DCHQ502926 - Picture courtesy of A P Knighton

Grand Theatre, Babington Lane. *The Grand Theatre, viewed in this picture from Gower Street, is now a restaurant, but you can still see the old name clearly above the entrance. It was built on land formerly occupied by the gardens to Babington House and was opened on the 25th March 1886, by Birmingham theatre manager, impresario and actor Andrew Melville. Disaster struck after six weeks, when the theatre was burned down with the loss of two lives. In a matter of only a few months it was re-built bigger and better than before. Over the next 64 years, it staged a wide variety of entertainment, including playing host to some of the biggest names in British entertainment. Unfortunately, the theatre had its limitations and despite a significant redecoration in 1948, it was not possible to expand the theatre's seating capacity, and little could be done to improve the general facilities in what was becoming a more demanding era. This led the Grand's proprietor, Prince Littler, to begin looking for something more suitable, and he acquired the Hippodrome in Green Lane and closed the Grand on the 9th December 1950.*

The cast of the 'A Greek Slave' at the Grand Theatre. *A c1904 postcard advertising a musical comedy called a 'A Greek Slave'. Many famous stars including Lillie Langtry, a renowned beauty, and former mistress of the then Prince of Wales, performed at the theatre. In 1922, Ivor Novello appeared in 'The Rat' and Max Bygraves made his review debut at The Grand. Frankie Howerd appeared well down the bill, returning at a later date as the star of the show. Perhaps the person most loved by the people of Derby was Gracie Fields, who performed a charity concert at The Grand in 1938.*

DMAG000127 - Picture courtesy of Derby Museums and Art Gallery

DMAG200168 - Picture courtesy of Derby Museums and Art Gallery

Babington House. *A picture of the east front, c1920 of Babington House, which was built in 1626 for Henry Mellor, later to become Derby's first mayor. Babington House was an imposing mansion, situated opposite to Babington Hall. It was entered from the street through a four centered 'Tudor' arch, decorated with three heraldic beasts set in the high perimeter wall. According to the hearth tax returns for 1670, it was the biggest single residence in Derby. Originally the house was known as St Peter's House, and set in 13 acres of parkland and flower beds. To the east it was bordered by Osmaston Road and the gardens of the old Babington Hall, where Mary Queen of Scots stayed on 13 January 1585. A plaque in St Peter's Street indicates where the hall once stood. Babington House has been replaced by Babington Buildings.*

DRBY004655 - Picture courtesy of Derby City Council

Brian Clough signing copies of his autobiography at Waterstone's. *Brian Clough was a football legend in his own lifetime. He began his football career at his home-town club of Middlesbrough, where he enjoyed considerable success, before moving to Sunderland FC. In total he scored 204 goals in 222 games and won two England caps, before his career ended prematurely due to a knee injury. He then turned to management where he enjoyed a spectacular rise to stardom. After a successful start at Hartlepool, Clough moved to Derby County, taking them to the Division Two championship and then the Division One title in 1972, but after a disagreement with the chairman he resigned. Two short unproductive spells at Brighton and Leeds United followed, before moving to Nottingham Forest in 1975 where he embarked on a hugely successful reign. Forest won the League Championship in 1978 and the League Cup in 1978 and 1979. There were successive European Cup triumphs in 1979 and 1980 and he later won the League Cup two further times with Forest. Clough was made a Freeman of Derby in 2003 and died on 20 September 2004.*

DRBY002468 - Picture courtesy of Derby City Council

Babington Lane. *This picture has been taken in the early 1950s, looking south from St Peter's Street up Babington Lane. On the left are Babington Buildings, designed by Methodist chapel architect John Wills for Hull-born entrepreneur Councillor G E Franklin. He was the proprietor of a national footwear chain called the Public Benefit Boot and Shoe Company, who had their branch on the ground floor and rented out the upper floors. The area until recently identified as 'The Lanes' was the place people went to be entertained, because as well as the Hippodrome and Grand half way between St Peter's and Gower Street, on Babington Lane was the Midland Electric Theatre/Picture House. It can just be picked out on the right, in the photograph. Opened on the 27 July 1910, it closed on the 27 August 1960.*

The Spot, St Peter's Street. *Since this photograph was taken in 1982, The Spot has been redeveloped as part of the City Council's Derby Promenade scheme of the 1990s. In addition the Eagle Centre, on the right of the picture has been replaced by Westfield. In 1993 as part of the redevelopment plan a clock tower was added and the underground toilet block became even less conspicuous than it had been. The Spot is a well known landmark, but exactly how it got the name is a curiosity as no one seems to know how it was derived, although there are several theories.*

DRBY003059 - Picture courtesy of Derby Evening Telegraph

DRBY005441 - Picture courtesy of Derby City Council

Crowds and King Edward VII watch the unveiling of the statue of Queen Victoria, The Spot. *King Edward VII visited Derby to unveil the statue of his mother, Queen Victoria, on the 28 June 1906. Originally located at The Spot, the bronze statue donated by the famous Derby Engineer, Sir Alfred Seale Haslam was moved to the grounds of the former Derbyshire Royal Infirmary. Queen Victoria made her only state visit to Derby in 1891, when she laid the foundation stone of the new Derbyshire Royal Infirmary, and during the course of her visit knighted the Mayor, Alderman Alfred Seale Haslam at Derby Railway Station. The shops behind the large crowds are Frank Woore (bookbinder), Mapperley Colliery Co Ltd's Order Offices, and Lancaster and Thorpe's opticians.*

St Peter's Street and Babington Lane Junction. *A very detailed, early 1900s view down St Peter's Street from The Spot, with two Derby Corporation Electric Trams heading off down the street. After Queen Victoria's statue had been re-sited, an underground toilet block was built in the area left vacant. In the 1750s, The Spot was the point from where the new London turnpike road diverged from the old route via Osmaston and Swarkestone Bridge. It is now a good place to get a slightly elevated view of the line of the ancient north – south trackway, which existed long before Derby came into existence.*

DMAG000183 - Picture courtesy of Derby Museums and Art Gallery

DRBY001244 - Picture courtesy of Derby City Council

St Peter's Church. *This c1906 photograph shows the exterior of the south side of the chancel. St Peter's Church is the oldest church in Derby and still contains some Saxon fabric. Precisely when St Peter's was founded is uncertain; but it was recorded in the Domesday Book and may go back much further. On the pillar at the north side of the chancel arch, and on the wall of the south aisle, are capital letters carved by Norman craftsmen. Much of the church dates back to medieval times, the arches, and between the central and side aisles, together with the windows in the south and north walls, all date back to that period. An ancient carved stone in the south wall is claimed to be a Saxon cross which used to stand in the old churchyard. The squint does not have anything to do with lepers as may have been first thought, but was used by the clergy to see the high altar from the first-floor vestry. The church celebrates its birthday every year on St Peter's Day and according to present day church thinking, it was founded in 1042.*

St Peter's Church-oak chest. *The Flemish chest, shown in this pre 1958 picture, which stands in the south aisle is reputedly a product of the 14th century. In 1349, St Peter's Parish was badly hit by the Black Death, and victims were buried vertically in the churchyard to save space. Both the vicar of St. Peter's and his chaplain of the Blessed Virgin were among those who lost their lives to the Black Death. Over 200 years later during a further outbreak of the plague, St Peter's Parish once again was severely hit. As a consequence the churchyard could no longer handle all the burials, and some were diverted for interment at Boulton Chapel.*

DRBY005474 - Picture courtesy of Derby City Council

DRBY007782 - Picture courtesy of Derby Evening Telegraph

Traffic on St Peter's Street. *This 1930s picture looking down St Peter's Street from near the Spot is a very busy one. It would have been much more difficult in those days to cross the road than it is today since the road was pedestrianised. Cars, a lorry, a bus and bycles are all jostling for space, while the pedestrians seem in no hurry to go about their affairs. In the foreground the tram lines can be seen to diverge. Edwards Glass and China shop can be easily picked out on the left hand side of the picture.*

St Peter's Street and Boots the Chemist's shop. *This picture was taken around 1900 and certainly before 1912, when Boots moved to a site on the corner of St Peter's Street and East Street. John Boot, born in Radcliffe on Trent, Nottinghamshire in 1815, founded Boots the Chemists 34 years later. It was his son, Jesse Boot, who transformed the company into a national retailer. The company branded itself as 'Chemists to the Nation', before Boot sold out his controlling interest to American investors in 1920. However, deteriorating economic circumstances in North America saw Boots sold back into British hands in 1933. In 2005, Boots and Alliance UniChem merged, the merger becoming effective on 31 July 2006.*

DRBY007925 - Picture courtesy of Derby City Council

DRBY001651 - Picture courtesy of Nigel Aspdin

St Peter's Street. *In this late 1800s picture of St Peter's Street a large crowd of people are seen watching the unloading of wooden tea chests from a long line of carts. Presumably the tea is being delivered to the Star Tea Company shop near the centre of the photograph. Robert Sangster's Grocers, Hurd and Dean Drapers, and John Eaton Outfitters are also shown. The horse-drawn trams with the original 1880 livery and large, ornate fleet numbers were operated by the Derby Tramways Company. The trams were built by the Starbuck Company of Birkenhead who supplied 16 to the Tramways Company.*

John Dean's Drapers shop. *The picture has been taken about 10 years after the one above, which shows the location of the shop in St Peter's Street. A name change has taken place from Hurd and Dean to John Dean. Photography was in its infancy in the early 1900s and it was quite an occasion to have your photograph taken. No doubt the owner of the shop, aware of the publicity value of a picture of the shop front, has gathered together his staff at in the doorway to the premises for the benefit of the photographer.*

DRBY001650 - Picture courtesy of Nigel Aspdin

DMAG001091 - Picture courtesy of Derby Museums and Art Gallery

East Street from St Peter's Street. *This 1925 picture shows the Midland Drapery on the left and the Boots the Chemists store on the right. Boots moved into the Arts-and-Crafts designed shop by Albert Bromley, which is one of the city's most appealing buildings, in 1912. What particularly draws attention to the building are the four small statues in niches spaced out above the shop frontage. The statues are of Florence Nightingale, the 'Lady with the Lamp', John Lombe a member of the family who established the Silk Mill, William Hutton who published a 'History of Derby' in 1791 and Jedediah Strutt, the first of a family of mill owner's and public benefactors. The Midland Drapery had a distinctive magnet symbol at parapet level at the corner. It was founded by Edwin T. Ann, who later became an Alderman, and was one of the largest department stores in the country, employing 300 people in 1909. The store closed in 1970.*

Old Grammar School, St Peter's Churchyard. *It is not known when Derby School was founded, or who founded it, but the first mention is in a charter of Darley Abbey when the canons went to their newly founded Augustinian Monastery in 1146. Shortly after the dissolution of the monasteries, a charter was passed in 1554, for a free grammar school to be built in Derby. As a consequence, the Tudor building in St Peter's Churchyard was erected, and used as a school for three centuries. During these years, it became one of the most successful smaller public schools in the country. Having served a variety of purposes, it was in the ownership of the local entrepreneur, Richard Felix, for thirteen years, and operated as a Heritage Centre. Felix did much to put Derby on the tourist map, particularly as a result of introducing 'Ghost Walks' and for his involvement with television. He played a leading role in the popular TV series, 'Most Haunted' for several years. The centre closed in October 2005 and the premises are now occupied by a hairdresser. The picture dates back to 1910.*

DMAG300099 - Picture courtesy of Derby Museums and Art Gallery

DRBY001688 - Picture courtesy of Derby City Council

Royal Visit of 16 July 1881. *St Peter's Street lavishly decorated for the Royal visit of Prince Edward, the Prince of Wales. He was carrying out the task on behalf of his mother, Queen Victoria, visiting both the town and Royal Agricultural Show. The Prince was a fun loving person, enjoying racing, sailing and shooting and was hugely popular with the public as the large crowds indicate. The Mayor of Derby, Alderman Abraham Woodwiss, laid on a sumptuous banquet for the Prince and Princess Alexandra and he also reportedly had a private siding built for the Royal train. As he was later knighted and also obtained a second term as Mayor, he probably considered the money he had spent a good investment. Queen Victoria died on the 22 January 1901, after which the Prince became King Edward VII. The picture shows the royal carriage accompanied by ceremonial guards.*

Hospital Day Parade. *The picture of the Hospital Day celebrations, in 1924, was probably taken in St Peter's Street. Hospital Day was an annual event to raise money for the Derbyshire Royal Infirmary. In the days before state subsidised medicine, Hospital Days were held up and down the country and contributed significantly towards the income of local hospitals. The events arranged usually had a carnival atmosphere. In this picture the coachman in the top-hat is A C Poulson, driving the King of the Parade in a decorated carriage, probably hired from Avery's livery stables, Curzon Street, for the day. In the background is P E Stevenson, gentleman's outfitters.*

DRBY006553 - Picture courtesy of Maurice.A.Poulson

DMAG001704 - Picture courtesy of Derby Evening Telegraph

Tram tracks and trolleybus in St Peter's Street. *Pictured in 1933/4 is Derby Corporation trolleybus number 133 climbing slowly up St Peter's Street, on service number 22 from Ashbourne Road (Kingsway) to the Midland Railway Station. Set in the road are the electric tramcar tracks which appear to be still in use at the time, although the introduction of trolleybuses would shortly lead to their abandonment. The trolleybus service shown, commenced operating in December 1933, and the tram tracks were finally dispensed with in June 1934. Trolleybus number 133 was a Guy BTX with Brush bodywork and was new in September 1933.*

Postcard of the Inauguration of Electric Trams. *The first electric tram routes came into service on the 27 July 1904 and later that year on the 8 September the routes terminating at The Spot were extended down St Peter's Street and into Victoria Street. A crowd has turned out to see one of the new trams in St Peter's Street decked with garlands and flowers. The electric trams replaced horse drawn trams, which had served the city for the previous 25 years. In 1930 the replacement of trams by trolleybuses was recommended. Gradually the conversion took place, with electric trams operating workman special services, until the 30 June 1934. The system was officially closed down on 2 July of that year.*

DMAG000677 - Picture courtesy of Derby Museums and Art Gallery

CHAPTER 3 - COUNCIL HOUSE TO WESTFIELD

Charles Aslin, who held the position of Derby Borough architect from 1929 to 1945, was involved in the Central Improvement Scheme in Derby. This covered an area from Exeter Bridge down to the Morledge, apart from the Council House; Aslin was also engaged in the building of Exeter Bridge, the Magistrates' Court and Police Station, the open market and the bus station as well as the River Gardens by the Derwent. Also, as part of the scheme, a new road, Corporation Street, was constructed and some existing roads were widened.

Construction of the Council House began in 1938, and was scheduled for completion in 1941, but on the outbreak of the Second World War, work stopped immediately. It was allowed to resume the following year and in 1942, with the building nearly complete, it was taken over by the Government for the war effort and was occupied by the Royal Air Force. They remained there until 1946.

The official opening of the Council House took place on the 27 June 1949, when the ceremony was performed by Princess Elizabeth and her husband, Prince Philip. The Princess was handed a silver gilt key by Alderman Raynes, with which she officially opened the building. However, the building was not fully finished and it was not until 21 October 1954, that the council chamber was finally completed and opened, by Alderman W R Raynes. This was a particularly symbolic date as Derby was celebrating its 800th anniversary that year, since Henry II granted Derby's first charter to hold markets and fairs in 1154. It was also the anniversary of the granting of a further charter, by Mary Tudor, in 1554.

For years market stalls lined the Morledge, until the land was acquired for the new bus station, which was opened in 1933. An outdoor market was then set up next to the bus station and was opened on the 5 May 1933 by the Mayor, Alderman A. Moult, when at that time it was one of the most up-to-date in the Midlands. It closed when the indoor Eagle Centre Market opened on 20 November 1975, amongst much controversy.

The Eagle Centre, when it was opened, provided Derby with its first large indoor shopping mall. Refurbishment followed, before it was eventually transformed over a three year period into the new Westfield Derby, losing its old name as part of the re-branding exercise. It opened to the public on the 9 October 2007. This eagerly awaited event saw 150,000 people come through the centre's doors in the first eight hours of trading. The busiest retail day in Derby's history!

Trail: The Council House – Full Street (detour) – Derwent Street – River Gardens – Bass Recreation Ground – Eagle Centre Market – Westfield – The Morledge.

View from the Cathedral tower. *This 1955 view was taken looking towards the Council House. The Old Assembly Rooms are pictured in the centre and the quadrangular design of the Council House can be easily picked out. A limited number of dates are set on one side every year for Cathedral Tower Climbs. These days are very popular with photographers, who in the age of digital cameras, often carry a much lighter load than their predecessors up the 189 steps. The view at the top of the climb over three counties is spectacular, which makes all the effort of climbing up the steps well worth while.*

DRBY005934 - Picture courtesy of Derby City Council

DRBY004647 - Picture courtesy of Derby Evening Telegraph

Rams players parade the League Championship trophy. *Crowds of Rams fans gather around the steps of the Council House in May 1972, when the Derby County players proudly paraded the league championship trophy for the first time in the club's history. Three years later, under the stewardship of Dave Mackay, the club repeated their success, again winning the league title. Prior to winning the league title for the first time, the club's major honour had been defeating Charlton Athletic 4-1 after extra-time, in the 1946 FA Cup Final. The club was founded in 1884 by Derbyshire County Cricket Club to try to generate more income. Initially the intention was to call it Derbyshire County Football Club, but the local Football Association claimed that was too long and it was shortened to its present name. Originally matches were played at the Racecourse Ground, the home of the cricket club. Until, in 1895, the club moved to the Baseball Ground, where they remained for 102 years, before moving to Pride Park. Another curiosity is how the club's former ground got its name, which originated from Sir Francis Ley's visits to America, where he became interested in baseball. He provided a 12 acre, Vulcan Sports Ground and club, for his workers in the 1880s, with a baseball ground located in one corner. The ground was first used by Derby County in 1892, again in 1893 and permanently from 1895.*

DRBY005865 - Picture courtesy of Derby Evening Telegraph

HRH Queen Elizabeth visits Derby during her Silver Jubilee. *Queen Elizabeth II chats to pensioners at the front of the Council House, on the 28 July 1977, on her visit to Derby, which marked the 25th anniversary of her ascension to the throne. It was a time of considerable celebrations for Derby, as after several other attempts to achieve city status had failed; at last the wish had been granted. City status had been awarded on 7 June 1977 and the Queen during her visit presented the 'charter scroll' or 'letters patent' in person, on the steps of the Council House to Mayor Councillor Jeffrey Tillett. Until then Derby had been one of the few towns in England with a cathedral, but without city status.*

Derby Corporation Omnibus Department outing outside the Council House. *This happy picture of a smiling group of smartly dressed ladies, thought to be staff of the Derby Corporation Omnibus Department, about to embark on an outing was taken about five years after the Second World War ended. The official opening of the Council House by Princess Elizabeth and her husband, Prince Philip took place on the 27 June 1949. Despite this the building was not complete and it was not until the 21 October 1954 that the Council Chamber was officially opened.*

DMAG001633 - Picture courtesy of Derby Museums and Art Gallery

DMAG200495 - Picture courtesy of Derby Museums and Art Gallery

Exeter House, Full Street. *This picture taken in 1853 is one of the earliest known photographs of Derby and was credited to a very youthful Richard Keene. As is the case with early Keenes, the photographer himself is in the picture, together with Constable Benjamin Fearn and a small boy, thought to be Nick Yeomans. At the time the house was the largest town house in Derby. It was built c1635-40 and enlarged by the Town Clerk who owned the building in the 1680s. It was later owned by Thomas Chambers, a London merchant in copper and lead, whose younger daughter married Brownlow Cecil, the 8th Earl of Exeter, from whom the house takes its name. On the 4 December 1745, Bonnie Prince Charlie and his rebel army marched into Derby. The following day a meeting took place at Exeter House, when Lord George Murray proposed a retreat. The majority of the other leaders agreed and Bonnie Prince Charlie was unable to change their minds and the return to Scotland began. Exeter House has been demolished, but the oak panelling from the walls is now on display at Derby Museum and Art Gallery. The former Full Street Police Station, currently awaiting redevelopment, stands on the site.*

DRBY002374 - Picture courtesy of Derby Evening Telegraph

Parade of the Worcestershire and Sherwood Foresters, Derwent Street. *The ceremonial parade featured above took place in 1982, with the regimental mascot named Derby, accompanying the soldiers. The original mascot marched over 3,000 miles with the soldiers and was present in six actions and received, with the rest of the Regiment, the India Medal. This can be seen in the Regimental Museum at Nottingham Castle and a replica is worn by his successor on ceremonial parades. It has been a tradition for the Regiment to have a ram as a mascot; all named Derby and numbered consecutively. Derby is given an annual period of leave on the Duke of Devonshire's estate, where eventually, after completing their period of service, all rams retire. Derby is paid in the form of sweets and other luxuries.*

DMAG001705 - Picture courtesy of Derby Evening Telegraph

Exeter Bridge, Derwent Street. *This picture taken in the early 1930s shows a Derby Corporation trolleybus travelling along Derwent Street towards Nottingham Road, over the reconstructed Exeter Bridge. The concrete bridge replaced an earlier stone bridge. It was opened on the 13 March 1931 by the Rt. Hon. Herbert Morrison MP. Exeter Bridge is a single span concrete arch traffic bridge over the River Derwent. In the background of this picture are the premises of Graham & Bennett, 'English and Foreign Timber Merchants', while the cleared site in the foreground will eventually be occupied by the Council House.*

The Royal Standard public house, Derwent Street. *This picture was taken nearly 19 years before the pub was boarded up in January 2007. This was not the end, however, as it re-opened in 2008, as The Brewery Tap at the Royal Standard, due to the efforts of Derby micro-brewery pioneer Trevor Harris. It was erected around 1862, when it was much smaller than at present. It was named after the Sovereign's personal flag, always flown when the King or Queen is personally present, and it is said that Queen Victoria herself once drank in the lounge bar. The grand father of Reg Parnell, the famous Grand Prix motor racing driver, held the licence early last century. Reg Parnell and his brother Bill ran a large transport business from the yard of the pub and later in Alfreton Road.*

DMAG200344 - Picture courtesy of Derby City Council

DRBY004430 - Picture courtesy of Derby City Council

Top: Old Bridge over the River Derwent, c1790

Canary Island was that part of the east bank of the Derwent bounded by the canal and the river and was the location of the gardens of the wealthy people who lived in Full Street. The problem was that to get to the gardens most families had to use St Mary's Bridge, which they considered an inconvenience. As a result the Binghams of Exeter House built a wooden bridge across the river and Erasmus Darwin who lived at 3 Full Street, constructed a hand–operated ferry. As the bridge served Exeter House, it was soon named Exeter Bridge and after Jedediah Strutt bought the house, it was opened up to the general public, but still remained in private ownership. After Strutt's death, the bridge was widened and later taken over by Derby Corporation, which, in 1810, proposed further improvements and opened it as a public road. After this had taken place it remained until 1929, when it was demolished and replaced by a single span concrete bridge designed by Charles Herbert Aslin of the Council Architect's Department.

Bottom: Derby from Exeter Bridge, c1800

DCHQ003068 - Picture courtesy of Derbyshire Local Studies Libraries

THE FOUR BAS RELIEF ENGRAVINGS ON THE CORNERS OF EXETER BRIDGE

DRBY000634 - Picture courtesy of Derby Evening Telegraph

Exeter Bridge Engraving plaque of Erasmus Darwin. *Erasmus Darwin born in Nottinghamshire in 1731, but his most important achievements came when he lived in Derby and its immediate surrounds from 1781 until 1802. As a doctor he was known and respected throughout the land and tried to pioneer free medical advice for the poor. He was probably the greatest visionary of his age and had success in many fields, the first to discover how clouds formed, and he was responsible for many inventions. He re-established the Derby Philosophical Society, where the greatest and most creative minds in the country could exchange ideas. In addition he was one of the most famous poets of his era. Darwin died in his study at Breadsall Priory in 1802.*

DRBY000633 - Picture courtesy of Derby Evening Telegraph

Exeter Bridge Engraving plaque of John Lombe. *John Lombe came to Derby from Norwich, where he was born in around 1693. He tried to assist Thomas Cotchett, a barrister and business man in perfecting a fine silk to rival that imported from Italy. The mission failed, Cotchett bowed out of the business and Lombe decided there was nothing else for it, but to go to Italy and acquire the jealously guarded secrets. He drew diagrams of the equipment and smuggled them back to Britain, inside bales of silk fabric. He assisted his half brother, Thomas, in setting up a Silk Mill, engineered by George Sorocold. He died in 1722, many believe poisoned by a woman sent by the Italians to exact revenge for stealing their secrets.*

DRBY000632 - Picture courtesy of Derby Evening Telegraph

Exeter Bridge Engraving plaque of William Hutton. *William Hutton was born in Full Street, Derby on 30 September 1723. He was raised in poverty, his father was a heavy drinker and his mother died when he was very young. However, he rose to become a man of eminence, as an historian, poet and business man. Apprenticed at the age of seven to Lombe's Silk Mill, where he worked a 14 hour day, he was so small he had to wear clogs with raised heels in order to reach the machinery. Later, he became an apprentice silk stockinger, but ran away to Birmingham and learned new skills. After setting up a bookshop in Southwell, he started to write, his autobiography giving an important insight into working class conditions in eighteenth century Derby.*

Exeter Bridge Engraving plaque of Herbert Spencer. *Herbert Spencer was born at 12 Exeter Row, Derby on 27 April 1820, later moving with his family to 31 Wilmot Street, off Normanton Road. He was trained as a civil engineer and contributed a report on flood prevention to Derby Town Council in 1842, which had it been acted upon would almost certainly have saved the people of Derby from the worst ravages of future floods. Spencer went on to achieve great fame for his works on philosophy. His major works were: Principles of Biology (1864 - 1867), Principles of Psychology (1870 - 1872), Principles of Sociology (1876 - 1896), Principles of Ethics (1892 - 1893). He died in Brighton in 1903.*

DRBY000631 - Picture courtesy of Derby Evening Telegraph

DRBY006244 - Picture courtesy of Derby City Council

Riverside Gardens. *This view of the River Gardens and Water Lily Pool in 1933 was taken the same year that they were opened to the public, although the official opening ceremony did not take place until the following year. The Council House was not built until several years later, but the market on the left was opened on 5 May 1933. The gardens have changed considerably from the original design, which included a large formal pond planted with lilies complete with two large bronze turtle sculptures. However, the turtles can still be seen in the ornamental pond in the grounds of Allestree Hall.*

The Long Bridge. *The photograph has been taken from an illustration of Long Bridge, looking south across the River Derwent from Exeter Street towards Cockpit Hill. The Long Bridge took the towpath of the Derby Canal across the River Derwent. It connected both arms of the Derby Canal on either side of the river. Canals were a very important factor in providing transportation for cotton and Walter Evans of the Boar's Head Cotton Mills at Darley Abbey was appointed treasurer of Derby Canal Company. Raw cotton arrived at the ports of London, Liverpool and Hull and was transported using inland waterways to its destination. The problem was the canal did not quite reach the mill at Darley Abbey and to avoid the weir at Derby, a short branch canal, called the Phoenix, was built. It had two locks, the White Bear Lock and the Phoenix Lock.*

DMAG000571 - Picture courtesy of Derby Museums and Art Gallery

Activity on Derby Canal. *In ancient times the River Derwent had been used for transport from the Trent, but it was winding and shallow in many places and silt was a constant problem. The Trent was little better. James Brindley, the great canal builder, had planned to link the Trent and Mersey Canal with Derby, but was prevented from doing so by vested interests. As a result nothing further happened until Benjamin Outram was eventually commissioned to build the canal, which was completed in 1796, providing Derby with reliable water born transport. The canal ran from the Trent and Mersey Canal at Swarkestone to Derby and Little Eaton, and to the Erewash Canal at Sandiacre. This picture of the Derby Canal dates back to 1893.*

The Bass Recreation Ground – Open Air Free Baths. *Michael Thomas Bass, MP for Derby from 1848 to 1883 was a generous local benefactor. He gave the land to the town in 1867, on which the Bass Recreation Ground now stands. Bass had purchased the three acre site, bounded by the river Derwent and Morledge mill stream, and formerly known as 'The Holmes', in 1866 to form Derby's second park. The open air swimming baths comprised of two baths, measuring 100ft x50ft and 129 dressing cubicles. Bass hired George Thompson as the architect for the complex, which eventually cost him £2,500, in addition to the £3,850 he paid for the recreation ground. The baths opened in 1873 and were destroyed after the Second World War.*

DMAG001998 - Picture courtesy of Derby Museums and Art Gallery

Former Midland Railway Signal Works. *The Midland Railway established a Signal Wozks in 1871, located on a narrow strip of land between the Derby and Sheffield main line and the River Derwent north of Derby Midland Station. This view was taken some 16 years after the works closed and production was transferred to Crewe, in 1932. It looks south-east across the river from the Bass Recreation Ground. In the mid 1970s plans were completed for the new Northcliffe House to take over the site and from the end of 1979 departments of the paper began to move to the new site. There was though a problem, as negotiations for the change of working conditions were not yet complete with one production union, and the paper found itself in its new home but unable to publish. In the week it took for the agreement to be reached; only some emergency bulletins were published. On 9 February 1981, the first edition of the Derby Evening Telegraph was printed at its new home.*

The Eagle Centre Market re-opening ceremony, after refurbishment. *The refurbished Eagle Centre was officially re-opened on 26 June 1992 by the Mayor, Councillor Harold Johnson, and City Leader, Nick Brown. The market had been first opened in November 1975, when it had been designed in a contemporary style, to provide a pedestrianised covered environment for all year round shopping. The original design was not popular with many shoppers who complained of 'getting lost' and the new design was much more traditional in nature, with the stalls set out in straight lines, with wide aisles to allow for easier access.*

DRBY007589 - Picture courtesy of Derby Evening Telegraph

DRBY002372 - Picture courtesy of Derby Evening Telegraph

Derby Playhouse entrance. *Derby Playhouse was offered the site in the Eagle Centre by the City Council, as part of the new shopping development. It was officially opened on 20 September 1975 by the Duke of Devonshire. The original Playhouse had opened as the Little Theatre in Becket Street, in a converted Church Hall in 1948. Four years later it moved to converted premises in Sacheverel Street. Surviving a major fire in 1956, it became an important part of Britain's regional theatre network. Arts funding increased considerably in the 1960s and 1970s enabling the theatre to afford purpose built premises in the Eagle Centre. Following a period of financial problems the theatre was forced to close, but re-opened again in 2009 under the control of Derby Live. Further changes to the running of the theatre were made in 2011.*

Westfield. *Three years after work started on the new Westfield Derby, previously known as the Eagle Centre, it opened its doors to the public on the 9 October 2007. The prestigious centre, with sleek floor to ceiling glass fronts, changing mood lighting and the logos of top shops visible from every angle, was an instant success with most shoppers. Housing more than 150 outlets spread over a total of 105,800 square metres of floor space, it has a 800-seater food court and a 3,700-space multi-storey car park on the roof. Two thousand eight hundred and fifty jobs were created and the development was expected to attract inward investment to the city from investors who previously would not have considered Derby.*

DRBY007907 - Picture courtesy of Lu Vernon

Illuminated Co-op Cow sign. *The famous 'Co-op Cow' was illuminated by neon and, following its erection in the mid-1950s, it became somewhat of an icon for local people. Founded in 1849, it was the second oldest cooperative society in the World. For nearly all of the 1990s the Co-op occupied most of Albion Street/Exchange Street and the society's main department store remains in Albion Street. The co-op offered a wide range of services and at the beginning of the last century there were 60 separate stores and departments in Derby. Customers were particularly attracted by the payment of 'divi', where shoppers received a share of the profits. The more they spent the greater was the reward.*

Derby Ram Statue. *The statue was created in 1994 by sculptor Michael Pegler. It is an eight-foot high sculpture in Derbyshire gritstone, erected at the corner of Albion Street and East Street, following the completion of pedestrianisation in the city centre. Derby County Football Club are known as the 'Rams' and the name has been used by other organisations. The ram has played an important role in Derby Regimental history since 1858, when it first became a mascot. According to military history, the commanding officer of the regiment saw a fine fighting ram tethered in an Indian temple yard. He instructed one of his men to acquire the ram, which was the beginning of a long, illustrious career for the animal. It was named Private Derby and marched 3,000 miles throughout central India, and was present in six actions. As a result he was awarded the 'India Medal with Clasp Central India'. In all, Private Derby fought in 33 battles without once being defeated. Since then, there has been an uninterrupted run of rams acting as Regimental mascots all called Private Derby and numbered in sequence. A ballad was written many years ago about the 'Derby Ram' who by tradition was huge and much larger than depicted by the sculptor.*

DRBY006322 - Picture courtesy of Eric Matthews

DRBY004357 - Picture courtesy of Derby City Council

Opening Ceremony at Derby Bus Station, Morledge. *Derby Bus Station was opened on 2 October 1933 and was designed by Charles Aslin, the Borough architect. It was Derby's best and most popularly used example of 'Art Deco' architecture. When the city council proposed the removal of the bus station, which was thought to be out of date for present day requirements, there was considerable opposition. The eventual outcome was that the bus station was demolished and a new development called River Lights was commenced. The bus station section of the new development was opened in March 2010.*

Market on the Morledge. *This picture was taken in the early 1930s, just prior to the erection of the bus station. An open market was set up in 1933, next to the bus station, when it moved from the market place, which lasted until the completion of the Eagle Centre. In this picture market stalls line the Morledge and the Power Station, Guildhall Tower and Cathedral Tower can be seen on the skyline. On the right of the picture is the site formerly occupied by the cattle market. One of the principal rights enshrined in the charter, granted by Henry II in 1154, was the consent to hold markets. As a result, weekly markets for the sale of livestock were held at the Morledge until 1861. The market then moved to the Holmes, until shortly after its centenary celebrations in 1962, when it gave way for the Inner Ring Road and moved to a purpose built cattle market on Chequers Road.*

DRBY004080 - Picture courtesy of Derby City Council

Morledge Pleasure Fair. *The photographer took this picture of the Market and Fair, from the Ice Factory in the Morledge. The fair was greatly reduced in size from former years, but was still eagerly looked forward to by the inhabitants of Derby. The shot tower and surrounding buildings had been demolished prior to this picture being taken to make way for Derby Bus Station. This was the last fair to be held there as once it was decided that the Morledge was to be widened and cleared, the stalls and charter fairs had to go.*

DRBY006061 - Picture courtesy of Derby City Council

The Noah's Ark Public House, Morledge. *Established in the first half of the 1700s, for 30 years the pub operated alongside another hostelry bearing the same name, until in 1873 the adjacent pub changed its name. The only concession made to avoid confusion before 1873 was adding 'Old' to the title, in 1852. This has now been dropped. The name probably originates from the story of coin-clipper and forger Noah Bullock who lived in an ark on the River Derwent. He was a 17th century gentleman and counterfeiter, who built an ark for himself and his family on the river; from where he carried out his illegal occupation. In 1676 his crime - a capital offence in those days - was discovered and he appeared before the Recorder for Derby, Sir Simon Degge. He knew Degge well and promised to end his criminal activities and destroy his ark, in order to escape the hangman's noose.*

DMAG001179 - Picture courtesy of Derby Museums and Art Gallery

The Shot Tower on the Morledge. *One of Derby's most famous landmarks used to be the Shot Tower. It was 149.5 feet high, 10 feet wide at the top and 27 feet 11 inches wide at the bottom. The Shot Tower was demolished in 1932 as part of the Central Improvement Scheme. It was built in 1809, about ten years prior to this picture, for the manufacture of lead shot, by Messrs Cox and Poyser, whose works covered most of the site from the early 1800s. The walls were 14 inches thick at the top and 3 feet 2 inches thick at the base and there were 196 steps covering a distance of 210 feet, the tower consisting of approximately 250,000 bricks. Molten lead was poured through a grille at the top of the tower, separating into globules and cooling as it descended, finally being cooled in a trough at the bottom. The shot was then loaded into cartridges at an isolated works in Littleover. The building still exists but is no longer isolated.*

DRBY004698 - Picture courtesy of Derby City Council

CHAPTER 4 - ST MARY'S ROMAN CATHOLIC CHURCH TO FRIAR GATE BRIDGE

There is much of interest, together with many fine buildings on the western side of the Inner Ring Road. St Mary's Bridge Chapel is one of only a few remaining in this country. St Alkmund's Well is one of very few holy wells still in existence in Britain. St Mary's Roman Catholic Church has been described as 'Pugin's Masterpiece' and the Georgian Group, of London, referred to St Helen's House as 'one of the finest and largest eighteenth century townhouses to survive in any provincial city'.

Friar Gate was designated, the first Conservation Area in Derby, in September 1969, and has been extended several times. It has many interesting buildings though it is best known for its fine Georgian buildings, which line the main street. Originally called Markeaton Lane, it takes its name from the 13th century Friary that once stood by the road in the lower part of Friar Gate. There was also a Priory of the Convent of St Mary de Pratis, located near Friar Gate. It gave its name to Nun's Street and Nun's Green, which once occupied a large area of land on the north side of Friar Gate from the Headless Cross as far as Ford Street. The upper end of Friar Gate was the site where horse and cattle fairs were held from early times until 1861, which explains the reason for the width of the street at its west end.

It was, though, for the executions that people flocked to the area during the 18th and 19th centuries, when the ritual procedures introduced by the Tudors became seen as entertainment for the masses. The executions outside the gaol at the bottom of Vernon Street attracted side shows, pedlars, acrobats and other entertainers. People even came by train for what some regarded as a good 'day out'. Local traders selling souvenirs did a roaring trade; there were gingerbread effigies of the prisoner to be executed. The more vile the crime and notorious the prisoner, the larger were the crowds. Some executions attracted crowds of 20,000 to 40,000 people.

Pickford's House at 41 Friar Gate is a handsome Grade I listed building, built in 1769 by Derby architect Joseph Pickford, for his own occupation. He was born in Warwick in 1734 and was the son of a stonemason. At the age of 14 he was apprenticed to his uncle, who was also a stonemason. After working on Horse Guards Parade in Whitehall and several other projects with his uncle, he became involved in 1759, with work at Foremark Hall in Derbyshire. Three years later he married and set up home in Derby and attracted a number of notable patrons, the Duke of Devonshire being the foremost. His most noteworthy achievement in Derby was designing St Helen's House.

St Mary's Bridge. *A 1958 view of St Mary's Bridge and its Bridge Chapel. The bridge is an impressive structure of neo-classical design built by Thomas Harrison of Chester, between 1789 and 1794. The original bridge pier can be viewed under the foundations of the chapel and other remnants of the medieval bridge are to be seen in the river. It is remembered as the place where the Padley martyrs remains were hung on the bridge outside the chapel, which at that time was serving as a gaol. They had been hung, drawn and quartered after being convicted of treason for their religious beliefs. The 'red' windows in St Mary's Roman Catholic Church show the six Derbyshire Martyrs, three of whom were the Padley martyrs, who died for their faith. St Mary's Bridge Chapel is one of only six bridge chapels left in England. It stands beside the 18th century St Mary's Bridge, which replaced a medieval bridge to which the chapel was attached. The precise date when the first bridge chapel came into existence is uncertain, but it was probably around the late 13th to the early 14th century, when it was built on the same site as the present chapel. At the time when the chapel was built, travel was a dangerous occupation with robbery and murder not uncommon and the bridge chapel offered spiritual reassurance to travellers. The chapel also served as a collection point for tolls levied on traffic entering Derby. It was the only crossing point of the River Derwent into Derby and it was the resident hermit's responsibility to collect the tolls on people and livestock crossing the bridge. The hagioscope, or squint, on the north wall would have been used by the hermit to monitor traffic, as well as by passers-by to see the light indicating the presence of the Blessed Sacrament. The chapel is open to the public for a number of days every year.*

DRBY006990 - Picture courtesy of Derby City Council

North Parade and Darley Lane. *This 1917 view looking down North Parade and Darley Lane shows Derby Cathedral (1927), St Mary's and St Alkmund's churches in the background. The land was sold to the North Parade Building Club between 1818 and 1822, when William Strutt began selling off parts of his St Helen's House estate. The properties have been built in two lots of eight on a falling site, which provides an extra storey at the rear. Ashlar faced and of substantial design, they were built by William Smith of Derby. North Parade, numbered one to sixteen, is a Grade II listed terrace. Most of the development behind St Helen's House, known as the Derwent Park Estate, took place in the 19th century. Edward Street was built in the 1840s; North Street and Henry Street in the 1850s. Belper Road, Ruskin Road and Chevin Road were laid out in 1879 but not actually built until the 1890s.*

DMAG200241 - Picture courtesy of Derby Museums and Art Gallery

St Alkmund's Well, Well Street. *Surviving Holy Wells are uncommon in this country and it is surprising to find Derby's last remaining Holy Well in a built-up area well away from the city centre. Located in Well Street, St Alkmund's Well, whose earliest mention was in 1190, may date back much further too shortly after 800. This was the time of the dedication of the first minster church of Derby to St Alkmund, the martyred son of the King of Northumbria. The ancient tradition of Well Dressing was revived in 1870, but discontinued in the 1960s, when St Alkmund's Church was demolished when the road was widened. However, the lid of St. Alkmund's coffin can still be seen in Derby Museum. The picture dates back to 1924.*

DMAG300064 - Picture courtesy of Derby Museums and Art Gallery

DRBY003854 - Picture courtesy of Derby City Council

St Mary's Roman Catholic Church. *The foundation stone for St Mary's Roman Catholic Church was laid on the 4 July 1838, Queen Victoria's Coronation Day. The church was built in less than 18 months without the aid of modern day construction techniques, and was completed by 9th October 1839. It was the first major church designed by Augustus W.N. Pugin, his rise to prominence having largely come about by five books he had published on ecclesiastical architecture. He expertly put theory into practice and the church became known as 'Pugin's Masterpiece'. At the official opening Doctor Wiseman (later Cardinal), said that: 'St Mary's, without exception was the most magnificent thing that Catholics have yet done in modern times in this country.' Unusually, the church has been built on a north/south axis and not the traditional east/west axis. This was due to the shape of the land and Pugin was careful to point this out in a book he wrote in 1843. He also informed those who criticised him that there was no alternative. The picture dates back to c1890 and shows the west front and tower as seen from St Alkmund's Churchyard. Part of St Alkmund's Church is also in the picture.*

New Year Mass at St Mary's RC Church. *Children are seen in this photograph lighting candles at midnight mass to celebrate the New Year, 1 January 1981. The addition of a Lady Chapel in 1853, which was said at the time to be the largest Lady Chapel in England has been the only major structural alteration since the church was built. However, there was a major alarm in 1927, when it was found that unless urgent repairs were carried out the tower was likely to collapse. Some of the stone slabs had been originally cut incorrectly and as, a result, the weather had penetrated the mortar pointing and the stone had deteriorated. Further major interior and exterior renovation took place in the late 1980s, the result of 150 years wear and tear.*

DRBY005843 - Picture courtesy of Derby Evening Telegraph

The Seven Stars Inn, King Street. *This picture of the Seven Stars Inn, which faces St Helen's House on King Street, dates back to the 1880s. It was built in 1680, but there is no record of it acting as a pub until 1775. Beer, brewed on the premises until 1965, was drunk out of china tankards instead of glasses, supplied by the old porcelain works nearby until 1945 when the supply of mugs ran out. Nobody is quite sure if the mugs ran out because they had been broken, or they had been taken away by drinkers as souvenirs. It is a Grade II* listed building and may at one time have been called The Plough.*

DMAG300061 - Picture courtesy of Derby Museums and Art Gallery

DRBY004008 - Picture courtesy of Derbyshire Libraries & Heritage

Derby Grammar School, St Helen's House, King Street. *St Helen's House, a designated Grade I listed building, was built in 1766/7, to the design of the Derby based architect Joseph Pickford, for Alderman John Gisborne, of Yoxall Lodge, Staffordshire. It has been described by the Georgian Group, of London, as 'one of the finest and largest eighteenth century townhouses to survive in any provincial city.' In 1803, it became the home of William Strutt and his son, Edward, and sixty years later of Derby Grammar School, after moving from their original premises in St Peter's Churchyard. The school moved out in 1967, after which the house was used for a time as an Art School and then for Adult Education. The steady deterioration of the house eventually led to its closure and it remained in the hands of Derby City Council for a number of years. In November 2006 it was sold to Richard Blunt, a developer with a good reputation as a restorer of threatened historic buildings. The picture was taken around 1920.*

Derby School, St Helen's House, King Street. *This picture is a copy of an early 1900s postcard of one of the class rooms at St Helen's House, by Buchanan of Croydon. Following the acquisition of the house for educational purposes, additional rooms were provided to commemorate the visit of the Prince and Princess of Wales. Also, in 1893, a chapel had been added and the school playing fields extended. Games were played at Parker's Piece, a small ground on the banks of the River Derwent and there was a boathouse for the rowing club. The school was evacuated during the Second World War, moving to Overton Hall at Ashover, until the end of the war. A few years after that the school moved again to Moorway Lane, Littleover.*

DRBY002368 - Picture courtesy of Derby City Council

DMAG300060 - Picture courtesy of Derby Museums and Art Gallery

Friends' Meeting House St Helen's Street. *In Simpson's book, the 'History and Antiquities of Derby,' the Quakers in Derby were referred to as one of the earliest establishments of that faith. The Friends' Meeting House was built in the early 1800s for the Quakers. It is believed to contain masonry of considerable antiquity from the old Hospital of St Helen. Previously The Quakers survived discreetly, relying on meeting in private rooms. George Fox, the founder of the Quakers, was imprisoned for blasphemy in the notorious town gaol, under the Town Hall, between 1650 and 1651. At his trial he bade the court 'To tremble at the word of the Lord'. To which the Justice, Gervase Bennet, responded by calling Fox and his supporters 'Quakers', a name that still remains. The Meeting House still survives almost unchanged to this day and pictured above in 1922.*

Brook Street Baptist Chapel, Brook Street. *The former Baptist Chapel, pictured in 1882, stood by the side of Bridgett's, South Mill (Rykneld Mills). It was built in 1802 as Derby's first Baptist Chapel, and enlarged in 1815. By 1842, it was proving too small for the increasing congregation numbers and the chapel moved into the converted town house of William Evans in St Mary's Gate. Four years later the Wesleyan Reformers started to rent the building, prior to eventual purchase. They continued to use the chapel and school rooms at the back until 5 May 2002, when the final service was held and the building closed as a place of worship. It has been listed as a Grade II building and is now used as a restaurant.*

DCHQ007358 - Picture courtesy of Derbyshire Local Studies Libraries

DRBY006349 - Picture courtesy of Derby Museum and Art Gallery

Rykneld Tape Mills from Lodge Lane. *A 1970 picture of Rykneld Mills an impressive group of four silk mills which for generations had found work for weavers of 'narrow fabrics' as they were once called. Built in 1830 by Thomas Bridgett, by the turn of the 20th century the company was one of the biggest employers in Derby. Following Bridgett's death in 1833, his relations continued the business until 1870. It was then taken over by William Able, an iron founder who ran the mills, until the Lilley family took control and introduced the name Rykneld Tean in 1929. The mills are listed Grade II* buildings and have recently been turned into apartments.*

DRBY006292 - Picture courtesy of Lu Vernon

Bank's Mill, Brook Street. *Built in the 1860s for John and William Rickard, it was one of the last silk mills built in Derby. In recent times the mill has been turned into studios by Derby University, who own and manage the site. The studios were set up to retain Graduate level skills in the creative industries in the Derby area. By creating easy-in/easy-out workspace studios, and business and professional development support, graduates were helped to earn a living from those skills, either as sole traders or businesses. The mill hosts periodic 'Open Days', when visitors can browse or buy a vast range of unique artwork, jewellery, glassware, photography, ceramics, textiles, sculptures, poetry and much more.*

DRBY003734 - Picture courtesy of Derby City Council

St John's Church, Bridge Street. *This c1843 view shows the West End exterior of St John's Church, which is now the only surviving Commissioners' Church in Derby. It was for many years the centre for community life in Derby's old West End. It has always had a good musical tradition and the choir still lead Sunday services and on other special occasions. In addition the choir also visits other churches and cathedrals, including Liverpool, Durham and Blackburn Cathedrals. Before St John's Church was built, the population of Derby had been expanding for some time and the Bishop of Lichfield recognised that the town needed an additional church. Fortunately a fund had recently been set up by Parliament to encourage church building, but it was subject to considerable restrictions. The decision to proceed by this course was accordingly made and the commissioners' paid £2,547 while an additional £4,300 was raised by public subscription. The land on which it was built was given by the Hurt family whose town house was in Friar Gate and it was designed by Francis Goodwin, who, at the time, was working on the County Gaol in Vernon Street. It was intended to accommodate 1,200 - 1,300 worshipers, with 650 free seats and in design is rather similar to King's College Chapel, Cambridge. The church was consecrated in 1828, when it became the first 'new' church in Derby to be consecrated since the Reformation.*

DRBY000729 - Picture courtesy of Derby Evening Telegraph

Headless Cross, Friar Gate. *As you turn left out of Brick Street into Friar Gate, a Headless Cross without a shaft and of medieval origin has been positioned close to the side of the road. The cross was transferred to the Arboretum when the cattle market moved from Friar Gate in 1861, but 118 years later it was returned close to its original position. It is said that it was once a complete cross, but that it lost its head long before the battle of Agincourt. During outbreaks of the plague all public gatherings were discontinued. Food stuffs were left near the cross by the local farmers, who would vigorously chew tobacco, while depositing their produce, as this was considered to act as a disinfectant against disease. The hollow in the top of the stone was filled with vinegar, which acted as a form of disinfectant for the coins that were immersed by the starving citizens of Derby, in payment for the food.*

DMAG300004 - Picture courtesy of Derby Museums and Art Gallery

The County Gaol (Derby Prison) Vernon Gate. *The Corn Market Gaol was demolished in 1756 and a new gaol was built on Friar Gate to hold a maximum of 29 prisoners ranging from debtors to those awaiting execution. This soon proved insufficient and a new county gaol was built on Vernon Street and the old prison returned to the Borough. The gaol in Vernon Street was designed by Francis Goodwin and opened in 1827.At that time, it was claimed to be 'One of the most complete prisons in England.' It was later strengthened and fortified with Martello Towers designed by John Mason of Derby, following the Reform Act riots. It was re-modelled again in 1880 and changed its name to HM Prison Derby in 1886.*

Greyhound Stadium, Vernon Gate. *The interior of Derby Gaol was demolished in 1928, leaving only the Curtain Wall and the imposing entrance. It had been a gaol for just over 100 years and during the First World War it served as a military prison. In 1933, the Preston Greyhound Association converted it into a Greyhound Stadium, but this closed in 1988, two years after the picture was taken. Following the closure the area was redeveloped in 1996 for mixed accommodation and business use.*

DRBY006272 - Picture courtesy of Derby Evening Telegraph

DMAG200450 - Picture courtesy of Derby Museums and Art Gallery

Friar Gate House School. *Friar Gate House, a three storey, ashlar fronted building dating from around 1793, was the residence of Thomas Cox of Grindlow, a lead merchant. On his death in 1842, the house became the home of his sister Hannah until she died in 1874, when it was acquired as the town residence of Charles Edmund Newton of Mickleover Manor. Following his death, the house was divided, with one half being made into a school, run by Miss Mary Hawkins. It was later extended and remained operational until 2010. The picture taken in 1989 is of an annexe of the old school.*

Girl pupils of Friar Gate House School. *This picture is thought to have been taken at the beginning of the 1990s, showing a group of girl pupils, all smartly dressed in their school uniforms who seem to be enjoying being photographed. Friar House School was originally a day school for girls and a preparatory school for boys. The school operated until closure in November 2010, when it was known as Friar Gate House School. It was an Independent school for children aged from three upwards. The school was quite small and normally had around 60 children on the register.*

DRBY006047 - Picture courtesy of Derby Evening Telegraph

DRBY002572 - Picture courtesy of Derby City Council

Friar Gate County Gaol. *This picture probably dates back to the early 1800s of Derby County Gaol on Friar Gate, which was opened in 1756. Prior to this the town gaol had been located on the Cornmarket for almost 200 years, alongside the Markeaton Brook. Although the gaoler's accommodation was at street level, the cells were at basement level. The brook was also the town's main sewer, inevitably the gaol suffered from the horrible stench. As a result, many prisoners died from disease and from flooding. Nevertheless, it survived for almost 200 years, when, following numerous complaints (and, no doubt, deaths from disease), it was decided to build a more substantial structure away from the town centre. At a meeting in 1755, agreement was reached to relocate the gaol outside the centre of Derby and a site at Nun's Green was chosen. This was one of the traditional execution places for Derby and it appeared an ideal place for a more substantial gaol to be built. In 1756, the Cornmarket gaol was closed and the new gaol had its first complement of prisoners. Designed to house a maximum of 29 prisoners, it was soon obvious that it was too small, but it was some years before another gaol was built.*

The south west side of the Derby County Gaol, Friar Gate. *A view of Derby County Gaol dated 1826. It is now a working museum which is open to the public having been acquired in 1997 by Richard Felix, paranormal investigator and dedicated historian. He later became famous as one of the members of the popular television programme 'Most Haunted'. The gaol was restored as far as possible to replicate its original state. Currently it has two cells: The Condemned Cell and the Debtor's Cell. Each one features the original doors which have been re-hung, complete with the prisoners' original 'graffiti'... names, dates and day markers, etched into the wood, marking down how many days the prisoner had until execution. A twenty four hour investigation in Derby by the TV's Most Haunted team brought both the gaol and the city to the attention of a wider audience and has resulted in it becoming a popular venue for ghost hunters.*

DRBY001749 - Picture courtesy of Derby City Council

The Greyhound Inn, Friar Gate. *The name of this late 17th century pub pre-dates the former Greyhound Stadium that used to operate in nearby Vernon Street, from where many people think it takes its name. The greyhound was a badge of Edward IV and, by inheritance the Tudor Monarchs and also the crest of two well known Derbyshire families, the Blackwalls and Gells. Originally thatched, the pub no longer owns the former carriage arch and adjacent buildings. During the period when cotton spinning was an important cottage industry, the landlord, Joshua Simmonds, sold stocking frames. It is one of only two remaining pubs that once served the animal markets that were held at the end of Friar Gate. Following closure in 2008, it was re-opened two years later by a well known Derby based brewery.*

DMAG300006 - Picture courtesy of Derby Museums and Art Gallery

Friar Gate. *This 1970 picture has been taken looking down Friar Gate, past Pickford's House on the left, to the railway bridge. Pickford's most notable achievements in Derby were the building of St Helen's House and his building work in Friar Gate, which was not just confined to the house he built for himself and his family. Designated in September 1969 and subsequently added to on several occasions, Friar Gate was Derby's first Conservation Area. The area has many interesting buildings, over 100 of which are listed as Buildings of Special Architectural or Historic Interest. It is best known for its fine Georgian buildings, but there are also a number of late Georgian and Regency buildings in Ashbourne Road, which are included in the Conservation Area.*

DRBY005791 - Picture courtesy of Derby City Council

DRBY004556 - Picture courtesy of Derby Evening Telegraph

Pickford's House Museum. *Pickford's House Museum, pictured in 1983, was built by eminent architect Joseph Pickford between 1769 and 1770 for his own occupation. The façade was designed to impress clients who might well only see the front of the house. For those who entered the premises, they would find the hall richly decorated with ornamental plasterwork and the house's finest room, the saloon, where they would probably be entertained, was entered by a door opposite the entrance. His builder's yard and stonemason's workshops are at the rear of the house. The house has been converted into a museum and was opened to the public in 1988.*

Royal Institution for the Deaf and Dumb, Friar Gate. *The Elementary Education Act of 1870 made free education available and all children under 12 were expected to attend school. This resulted in several Board Schools being opened in Derby. Deaf and dumb children were also catered for when William Roe at the age of 20, spent much of his spare time teaching uneducated deaf adults at his father's house. His reputation as a teacher of the deaf grew and his work became so time consuming that he started to work on a full time basis. In 1880, he, along with the Derbyshire Association for the Deaf, began raising funds to build a dedicated institution in Derby and a site was acquired on Friar Gate and the building completed in 1894. The picture is c1900.*

DMAG200071 - Picture courtesy of Derby City Council

Midland Deaf and Dumb Institution.

Friar Gate, Derby, 189

DRBY003245 - Picture courtesy of Derby City Council

The Midland Deaf and Dumb Institution. *This c1888 view is taken from an advertisement which also includes details of silver medals awarded at the Corporation Fine Art Exhibitions of 1887 and winter 1888. The Hon. Secretary is named as H H Bemrose Esq. and the Head Master as W R Roe. The caption below says 'View of New Institution being erected by Voluntary Contributions, for the completion of which the sum of £6,000 is still required.' The 'Royal' title was added after Queen Victoria's visit in her Diamond Jubilee year. In 1972 the school relocated to a site further out of town on Ashbourne Road and shortly afterwards the Friar Gate premises were demolished.*

DMAG001203 - Picture courtesy of Derby Museums and Art Gallery

Electrical transformer kiosk, Friar Gate. *This kiosk is somewhat of a mystery item for many passers-by who wonder what purpose it serves. It is actually an electrical transformer box. It was manufactured by Walter MacFarlane and Company of the Saracen Foundry, Glasgow, and formed part of Derby's original electrical lighting scheme of 1893 and is now preserved in situ. The kiosk has the 'Buck in the Park' emblem on the side. Now Derby's coat of arms, 'the Buck in the Park' first appeared on a medieval seal in 1446. Another surprise for many passersby is that the telephone kiosk by Friar Gate Bridge, known as K6, is Grade II listed. It was designed by the famous architect Sir Giles Gilbert Scott, the grandson of Sir George Gilbert Scott, who won a competition in 1935 for the design of telephone kiosks.*

DRBY006550 - Picture courtesy of Derby City Council

The Old White Horse Inn, Friar Gate. *This picturesque old pub with a thatched roof, and reputedly cruck-beamed, served the cattle and beast market a short distance away to the east, at the top end of Friar Gate. Unfortunately, it found itself on the line of the railway bridge that the Great Northern Railway was having built to carry the tracks over Friar Gate. As a result, the railway company acquired and demolished the pub in 1876. At the time of its demise it was thought to be the oldest pub in Derby. The picture dates back to around 1860.*

Railway Bridge over Friar Gate. *It is actually two bridges side by side, set at a slight angle to each other where the tracks diverged, to embrace the island platform of Derby Friargate Station (in this context 'Friargate' was always spelled as one word) off to the left. As the tracks were above the road, the Great Northern Railway Station was entered from below, and access was gained to the four platforms via a tunnel and steps. The first train left the station on the 1 April 1878 and the last on 5 May 1964. The final goods train passed through on 4 May 1968. The bridge was built by Handysides, a local Derby company. By the time this photograph c1940 was taken the GNR had become part of the London & North Eastern Railway, hence the initials painted on the bridge arch.*

DMAG001966 - Picture courtesy of Derby Museums and Art Gallery

DRBY006343 - Picture courtesy of Derby City Council

Friar Gate Bridge, Derby. *A c1900 picture of the ornamental bridge over Friar Gate, which carried the Great Northern Railway's Nottingham to Derby line. The GNR Company had Friar Gate Bridge constructed in 1878, despite very strong opposition. Local people were in uproar saying that the bridge would completely destroy the appearance of what they termed 'the best street in Derby,' anger only equivalent to that a century later when it was suggested the bridge should be removed. The bridge was made deliberately ornate to try to match the handsome Georgian street below and placate the protesters. It was built to serve Friargate Station, by the well-known Derby Engineering Firm of Andrew Handyside and Company Limited. The GNR line passed through the heart of the town. Property had to be demolished and residents uprooted, bridges built, cuttings embankments and a long viaduct constructed. Despite strong opposition, the GNR managed to get Parliament to pass an act to give them the go ahead in July 1872. They argued that the houses to be demolished were of poor quality and needed to be replaced, but the main reason people lived in the area was that they were poor and there were few other alternatives. In all a total of around 265 houses were demolished. Cherry, Short and Baxter streets were demolished entirely, and Granville and South Street shortened.*

Derby's Crest on Friar Gate Bridge. *As part of the ornamentation on Friar Gate Bridge, the borough crest or common seal of Derby, the Buck in the Park, is displayed. It depicts a deer, in the shape of a buck in a fenced park. Deer were in plentiful supply in Derbyshire when the Danish invaders named their first fort after the wild deer that were so abundant in the area. However, the crest was only officially sanctioned as a Coat of Arms in 1939. Apart from deer, sheep were the backbone of farming in the past and the ram is the county's regimental mascot.*

DRBY003267 - Picture courtesy of Mr M E Burrows

CHAPTER 5 - DERBY CATHEDRAL QUARTER – TRAIL 1

The Silk Mill stands on the site of the Lombe Brothers' mill, England's first modern factory and now part of the Derwent Valley World Heritage Site. It was John Lombe, who together with his half brother, Thomas, who set up the Silk Mill. He died in 1722, many believe poisoned by a woman sent by the Italians to extract revenge for stealing their secrets.

The patent for the 'Italian' machine was held by Thomas Lombe for 14 years, but when he attempted to renew the patent in 1732 Parliament refused the application. However, he did receive compensation, in return for which he was required to place an accurate model of the Silk Throwing Machine in the Tower of London for inspection. The silk industry in Derby continued to expand and by 1838 there were a total of 17 silk mills operating in the town. The largest factory in Bridge Street employed 750 people.

A mural takes up the whole of one of the external walls of the Silk Mill public house. It was painted in 1986 and depicts the Silk Trades' Lockout of 1833/4, when hundreds of newly-joined trade unionists found themselves locked out because of their membership of the Grand National Consolidated Trade Union. When the strike pay ran out, the strikers began to drift back to work. On Monday, 21st April 1834, the final strikers asked to be re-instated, although over 600 found their services no longer required.

All Saints Church became Derby Cathedral by Royal Charter in 1927, which was somewhat unusual as Derby was only a town at the time. It was founded prior to the Norman Conquest, but no trace exists of the original church. The tower completed in 1532 is the second highest in England. The Baroque nave was designed by James Gibbs and built by Francis Smith of Warwick in 1723-5. The magnificent wrought iron chancel screen and gates are the work of Robert Bakewell.

Iron Gate derives part of its name from the arrival of the Vikings in 874. Their language, alongside Saxon and English, would have been spoken for many generations. The suffix 'gate' is from the Norse word geata, which meant street in their language. Iron Gate used to be regarded as the Regent Street of Derby and still retains an important role in the life of the city. In the 1700s the street was described as 'consisting of inns and shopkeepers' and this still applies today.

The Quad. *The Quad centre opened in September 2007. It is an £11 million purpose built centre for art and film, with a gallery, two cinema screens, café bar and workshop that anyone can use. The BFI Mediatheque, a digital jukebox, enables visitors to view some of the rarest and most amazing films from the National Archive. After becoming a member, visitors simply log on at one of the viewing stations and choose what they want to watch without incurring any charge. You can journey back in time and view Victorian and Edwardian Britain or watch feature films. For those interested in local history there is a special archive collection.*

DRBY000846 - Picture courtesy of Derby City Council

Former Magistrates' Court, on the corner of Full Street. *A 1950s view looking towards the former Magistrates' Court with Exeter Bridge on the right. The Magistrates' Court was completed in 1934 as part of the Central Improvement Scheme, which also included the council house, the river gardens, an open market and a bus station. The designer was Charles H Aslin, who held the position of Derby Borough architect, from 1929 to 1945. A police station was also included on the northern side. Both buildings are currently awaiting re-development. The Magistrates' Court is a Grade II listed building.*

Derby from Derwent Bridge. *This 1909 view of the River Derwent shows industrial buildings lining the riverbank with the Silk Mill in the background. The Derwent rises at Swains Greave between Bleaklow and Howden Moors. It flows south through Derbyshire for its entire journey before merging with the River Trent at Shardlow. More than any other river its waters have played a vital part in driving mill machinery, placing Derbyshire at the forefront of the Industrial Revolution. In December 2001, the 15 mile stretch of the Derwent Valley from Matlock Bath to Derby was designated by UNESCO as a cultural World Heritage Site. The citation states: 'The cultural landscape of the Derwent Valley is of outstanding significance because it was here that the modern factory system was established to accommodate the new technology for spinning cotton developed by Richard Arkwright. The insertion of industrial establishments into a rural landscape necessitated the construction of housing for the workers in the mills, and the resulting settlements created an exceptional industrial landscape that has retained its qualities over two centuries.'*

DRBY004808 - Picture courtesy of Derby City Council

DRBY000389 - Picture courtesy of C B Sherwin

The Old Silk Mill Public House, Silk Mill Lane. *The first records of the existence of the Old Silk Mill pub by name are dated 1874, but it is likely that it dates back much further to the years when Sir Thomas Lombe's historic Silk Mill was fully operational. The old inn was demolished in 1924, shortly after this picture was taken, and replaced on a slightly different site by the present mock half-timbered building. A mural takes up the whole of one of the external walls. It was painted in 1986, depicting the Silk Trades' Lockout of 1833/4, when hundreds of newly-joined trade unionists found themselves locked out because of their membership of the Grand National Consolidated Trade Union. In November 1833 a silk manufacturer sacked a man who refused to pay a fine for poor workmanship. This resulted in eight hundred workers going on strike in support of their colleague. Other mill workers followed, and the employers retaliated by refusing to employ any union members. By February of the following year this figure had risen to over 2,000, while the owners kept the mills running with unskilled non-union labour. Strike pay ran out in March, and strikers began to drift back to work. On Monday, 21st April 1834, the final strikers asked to be re-instated, although over 600 found their services no longer required.*

Derby Power Station and Silk Mill from the River Derwent. *The banks of the river Derwent above Exeter Bridge, c1960, showing the Silk Mill and the massive Electric Power Station, partly sited on what is now Cathedral Green. It was originally built in 1893, with the addition of a 'New' boiler house in 1921, on the site of the 1778 Devonshire Hospital. The location of the Power Station, in such a sensitive spot, so close to the Cathedral and the centre of town was much criticised at the time of its construction. The older part of the Power Station was demolished in 1963-4 and a large substation constructed on the site. The remainder of the Power Station was eventually closed in 1969 and the site was cleared in 1972 to be replaced by an area of open space.*

DMAG200484 - Picture courtesy of Derby Museums and Art Gallery

DERBY SILK MILL

The Silk Mill with its eye catching Italian-style tower is a significant landmark in the city. Photographs of it must have appeared in more books and tourist guides about Derby than virtually any other location. Now it forms part of the Derwent Valley World Heritage Site.

The Chinese started to manufacture silk 3,000 years ago. Lovely to the eye and feel, silk has been in demand ever since it was first discovered. Silk production eventually reached Europe and it was the Italians who developed a fine silk thread and gained a monopoly in its manufacture. There was considerable demand for silk in this country, but the raw materials had to be obtained from China or Italy making it a very expensive commodity. The Italians closely guarded their secret method of production and all the initial attempts to match them failed.

In 1702, Thomas Cotchett, a solicitor from Mickleover, became interested in the potential commercial rewards of silk thread manufacture using water driven machinery. He entered the market and asked George Sorocold to build him a mill on an island site, on the banks of the River Derwent. The mill that Sorocold built for Cotchett, which later became known as 'The Old Shop', used 'Dutch machines', but the project was not successful. On the verge of bankruptcy, Cotchett withdrew, but John Lombe, one of Cotchett's employees was determined the venture would succeed. Despite the risks involved he went to Piedmont in Italy, where silk production was at the forefront, to both work and spy. He drew diagrams of the equipment and smuggled them back to Britain, inside bales of silk fabric.

Assisted by his half brother, Thomas, he set up the Silk Mill, which was built in 1717-8 by George Sorocold. He died in 1722, many believe poisoned by a woman sent by the Italians to exact revenge for stealing their secrets.

DRBY000519 - Picture courtesy of C B Sherwin

Silk Mill Gates. *This picture was taken in 1920 and shows the gates made by Robert Bakewell on the bridge leading to the Silk Mill. The mill was built near the site of Sorocold's earlier 1702 mill. It was rebuilt in 1821 and again after a fire in 1910. Only the carrying arches and the bell tower remain from the 18th century structure. The tower only acquired its present appearance after, it would appear, the 1821 fire, although some of the brickwork seems to be original. The Silk Mill housed Derby's Museum of Industry and History from 1974, before closure in 2011, but with the promise that it would reopen at some time in the future.*

DMAG001416 - Picture courtesy of Derby Museums and Art Gallery

Millstream, St Michael's Mills and Lombe's Silk Mill. *An 1874 view looking north from Silk Mill Lane up the millstream beside Lombe's Silk Mill, towards St Michael's Mills. From left to right the buildings are the three storey corn mill of W and G Brown, dating from c 1830; the gabled 17th century St Michael's Mills (corn) on the little 'Bye-flat' island; on the long 'Bye-flat' island on the right are the much re-built original silk mill erected by Thomas Cotchett in 1702; and the five storey Lombe's Silk Mill.*

The Silk Mill. *This postcard available for purchase in the 1890s shows the exterior of the Silk Mill with the River Derwent in the foreground. The main building shown is the Doubling Shop. It partially collapsed in September 1890 and was demolished. The Power Station and All Saints' Church (later Derby Cathedral) can also be picked out.*

DRBY004761 - Picture courtesy of Derby City Council

DRBY006730 - Picture courtesy of Derby Evening Telegraph

Pickfords Van (Registration R 1559) outside The Silk Mill – Derby's Museum of Industry and History. *The Silk Mill shown in the picture housed Derby's Museum of Industry and History, until April 2011, when it was closed for an indefinite period. It was the first factory in England where all the processes were carried out under one roof and utilising one source of power and is now a World Heritage Site. The foundations and part of the tower from the 1717 mill, built by George Sorocold, are still visible. Inside the museum the absorbing history of the Silk Mill was told in considerable detail. The museum also gave special emphasis to the development of Rolls-Royce aero engines and the railway industry. In addition, there were a number of other displays covering local industries, including mining, pottery and foundry work. The picture was taken in 1987.*

Cathedral Green. *The area now known as Cathedral Green was once the home of Derby Power Station. It was built late in the 1800s, when electricity was starting to become a proven alternative to gas. The power station continued to increase its capacity and in 1928 the Borough Council passed a proposal for the creation of a 'super-station'. This allowed Derby to meet all its requirements without having to buy power from elsewhere. Following the change from coal to oil, the power station was demolished in the early 1970s. After remaining as a grass covered open space for many years, the green has been redesigned to make the area more visitor friendly. An events area and a footbridge across the river are included in the improvements.*

DRBY005007 - Picture courtesy of Lu Vernon

'Bonnie Prince Charlie' statue. *The bronze equestrian Bonnie Prince Charlie Statue on the green was presented as a gift to the city by the late Lionel Pickering, a local benefactor. It was the first equestrian statue to be created anywhere in Britain since the Second World War and celebrates the 250th Anniversary of the '45. Following the arrival of Bonnie Prince Charlie and his Jacobite army in Derby on the 4 December 1745, an important decision in British history was made. On the previous day, the Prince had been advised by his generals to withdraw and return to Scotland. They were not happy being so far into enemy territory, without the expected support of the English Jacobites and doubtful that the planned French invasion to support the venture would take place. The decision to withdraw was made against the wishes of the Prince, who wanted to continue. London was in panic and had the march continued the path of British history could well have been changed.*

St Michael's Church, Queen Street. *This picture was taken prior to the rebuilding of the church in 1857–8, after the east gable collapsed during a service in 1856. John Erskine Clarke, who had just been appointed vicar, set about the task of organising the reconstruction. He was a man of considerable energy and skill and during his time at the church, he started what was regarded as the first church parish magazine ever to be published. Distressed at the violence he saw depicted in some children's comics, he founded 'The Prize' a magazine for young children. This was successful as was the 'Chatterbox', a halfpenny weekly paper aimed at older children. The church closed in the 1970s, having been in existence from at least the 11th century, along the ancient north–south route.*

DRBY006183 - Picture courtesy of Derby City Council

St Michael's Church, Queen Street. *A c1850 view of the interior of St Michael's Church, which since its closure in the 1970s has been sympathetically converted into architect's offices by Derek Latham. In the 17th and 18th centuries the churchyard contained the cistern to George Sorocold's ingenious system of providing drinking water to the townspeople of Derby. He had a very large pumping engine built, which was mounted on a moveable frame that rose and fell as the river levels changed, enabling water to be supplied on a regular basis. The water then went from the cistern and was circulated by gravity around the town in wooden pipes.*

DRBY004020 - Picture courtesy of Derby City Council

DCHQ502965 - Picture courtesy of A P Knighton

St Alkmund's Church, Queen Street. *A c1890s view of St Alkmund's Church, built in 1846, on the site of an earlier church. The church is claimed to have been originally founded early in the ninth century when St Alkmund's remains were bought to Derby. There are only six churches in England dedicated to him. Joseph Wright the internationally famous artist was buried there. The Church was rebuilt by H I Stevens at a cost of £7,700 and was demolished in 1967 in order to build the Inner Ring Road now called St Alkmund's Way. The original Nottingham Castle [Inn] was built c1550, but the building in this picture was erected in the 18th Century. It finally closed in 1962. A plaque close to the entrance of Jurys Hotel marks the site of the former church.*

John Smith Clock Works, Queen Street. *It was once a house, which was refronted by Joseph Pickford in 1764 for his friend the philosopher and clockmaker John Whitehurst. Later it was let to Joseph Wright and following his death it was divided, the left part becoming the Acorn Vaults, and the other Smith's Clock Works. John Smith a former apprentice of John Whitehurst III, had started his own business in Nuns' Street six years before moving to Queen Street. The firm has maintained an excellent reputation for clock making and repair over the years and as a result it has grown into one of the largest feature clockmakers in Europe. It was selected to make the clock for the Harmony Tower, to form the centerpiece of a new time theme park in China. At just over twice the size of Big Ben, it is the largest clock in the World. The firm now operates from a factory on Alfreton Road Derby.*

Shops, car tyre centre and the Flower Pot pub on King Street. *On the right in this 1970 picture is the Flower Pot public house. Built about 200 years ago it was originally a three storey house. The pub's name came as a result of Flower Shows held in nearby Cherry Street Drill Hall. During its earlier years it acted as a coaching inn, when there was room for 10 horses and wagons in the stables. The pub, having been extended into the property next door, is deceptively spacious inside. It is both a real ale and music venue, but the latter is kept separate to provide an area of comparative peace and quiet. The unusual sign is listed in a review of curious pub signs in the Midlands.*

DRBY005380 - Picture courtesy of Derby City Council

King Street Methodist Chapel Sunday School. *In 1805, the Methodists moved from St Michael's Lane and built a new chapel on King Street. The picture was probably taken around 1960 and is of King Street Methodist Chapel Sunday School, which replaced the previous building in 1841. Derby Dance now occupies the site and is the only dedicated dance house in the East Midlands, providing two dance studios, conferencing facilities, a café bar and two distinct performance spaces.*

DRBY001721 - Picture courtesy of Derby Evening Telegraph

Queen Street Swimming Baths. *Derby Borough Architect Herbert Aslin designed Queen Street Baths, which were opened to the public on 30 July 1932, by the Duke of Devonshire. The town's first public baths had been opened nearly three-quarters of century previously on Full Street, and had been followed 15 years later by the Reginald Street Baths. A growing population and the lack of bathing facilities at many homes, as well as the desire to swim, resulted in considerable demand being built up for a modern complex. The facilities included two pools with modern water purification, steam heating and ventilation systems. In 1962, a teaching pool was added and other improvements have been made in recent years. The picture dates back to pre-war days.*

DRBY007578 - Picture courtesy of Derby City Council

DRBY005083 - Picture courtesy of Derby City Council

Iron Gate from the Market Place. *This 1866 view was taken before the street was widened, in 1869, by the demolition of the shops and inns on the eastern side of the street and rebuilt over a period of twenty years. H I Stevens, George and Edwin Thompson and G H Sheffield all contributed one or more shops in a wide variety of styles. In the 1700s, the street was described as 'consisting of inns and shopkeepers' and this still applies today. It remains one of the principal streets in Derby with a mix of quality shops, pubs, cafes and restaurants, personal and professional services. It is the home to Bennett's, Derby's prestigious independent departmental store.*

The Old Dolphin Inn, Iron Gate. *The Dolphin is Derby's oldest surviving pub, claimed to have been founded in 1530. It is a fine example of a timber-framed building. The Dolphin was a well known Christian symbol in medieval days, which gives credibility to the presumed date of the founding of the pub. An old coaching inn, it is said to have been a stopping-off point for highwaymen including Dick Turpin. The pub's 18th-century extension at the rear was originally a doctor's house. Here he dissected bodies, using criminals who had been hung. According to folklore, one morning the doctor went down into his cellar after a body had been delivered and on pulling off the shroud found the person under it still clinging to life. Exactly what happened then is not known.*

DRBY004524 - Picture courtesy of Derby City Council

Derby Cathedral Centre, Iron Gate. *The Cathedral Centre was opened by HM the Queen on her visit to Derby on the 14 November 2003. Inside, there is a coffee shop and bookshop and at the rear a garden planted to represent a journey through the life of Jesus. Treasures from the Cathedral are displayed in the basement, together with ever-changing art exhibitions. The Coffee Shop, on the ground floor, serves light lunches, sandwiches, cakes and a wide range of tea and coffee; it sources most of its supplies locally. The highly acclaimed cafe was the winner of the Best Tea/Coffee Shop in the 2004 Derbyshire Food and Drinks Awards.*

The College, College Place. *This picture of The College, in College Place, which tends to hide away on the western side of Derby Cathedral, was drawn in 1929. It is a large townhouse which was built on the site of the former home of canons of the pre-reformation College of All Saints. The canons, together with other minor clerics, assistants and domestics lived in the buildings. The present day building contains remains of 17th century brickwork, but largely dates back to 1750s. It was altered to Regency style by Tory MP Daniel Parker Coke in 1808 and is now used for offices.*

DMAG300081 - Picture courtesy of Derby Museums and Art Gallery

DRBY004524 - Picture courtesy of Derby City Council

All Saints Church, Iron Gate. *Visible from a considerable distance, Derby Cathedral dominates the skyline with its impressive perpendicular tower, seen here in this c1890s photograph. It was built early in the 16th century, but worship has taken place on this site since the tenth century. Light and spacious inside, the iron screen by Robert Bakewell is an inspirational masterpiece in this proud and beautiful building. A combination of events led to it becoming Derby Cathedral, in 1927. In 1884, a new diocese of Southwell was created and the majority of the County of Derbyshire was transferred from Lichfield to the new see. Five years later, the first assistant bishop to the diocesan Bishop of Southwell was appointed with the title Bishop of Derby. He and his successor worked with the first Bishops of Southwell for the creation of a new diocese of Derby, and this was bought to fruition with the hallowing of All Saints as its Cathedral Church. In 1978, the outer part of the Cavendish burial vault was converted into a small Crypt Chapel. The cathedral houses many interesting features and monuments, including Bess of Hardwick's Monument, Joseph Wright's Tombstone, the Bakewell Screen and much more. The Cathedral Church of All Saints is exceptionally beautiful inside and the experience can be extended by visiting the Cathedral Centre on the opposite side of the road to admire some of the cathedral's treasures and to take refreshment. This view was probably taken from the window of Richard Keene's studio on Iron Gate.*

DRBY005820 - Picture courtesy of Derby Evening Telegraph

DRBY000944 - Picture courtesy of Derby Evening Telegraph

1 Left - Korean Veterans Association Service at Derby Cathedral, September 1982
2 Right - Spirit of Derbyshire Lifeboat Appeal Ceremony, 1990, when the Duke of Kent visited for the ceremony.
3 Below - Cathedral Choir Group, April 1991.

DRBY002384 - Picture courtesy of Derby Evening Telegraph

DRBY004365 - Picture courtesy of Derby City Council

Ring of Ten Bells, Derby Cathedral. *The tower at 212 feet is said to be the second highest in England, next to Boston Stump, and it has the oldest ring of ten bells in the world. Ancient records indicate that there were five bells at All Saints as long ago as 1509 and an additional five were added later. The bells were re-tuned and re-hung by John Taylor and Co. in 1927, when they were set down six feet or so lower in the tower, to minimise the danger of further damage through vibration. This was the year a new diocese of Derby was established with the hallowing of All Saints as its Cathedral Church on the 28th October 1927. In 1745, the Young Pretender is known to have ordered the bells of All Saints to be rung and to have attended with his officers a service held in the church. The photograph was taken at Taylor's Foundry at Long Eaton in 1927.*

Derby Local Studies Library, Iron Gate. *Set back from the road, under an archway, next to Pizza Express, is Derby Local Studies Library, where there are over 100,000 items available to consult within the library. Small selections of items are available for visitors to browse, but the main collection is 'behind the scenes' and is available on request. Many of the items have been donated like personal diaries, letters and photographs. There are microfilm machines to view newspapers and census details, and microfiche machines to examine the index of births, deaths and marriages. Derby Local Studies Library has been located here since 1985, previously the premises had served as a Police Station, Electricity Offices, and a Driving Licence Centre. The staff are very helpful and are readily available to assist your search for information. The library is scheduled for relocation.*

DRBY005151 - Picture courtesy of Derby City Council

DMAG300047 - Picture courtesy of Derby Museums and Art Gallery

Twenty-four Iron Gate. *This pre 1936 picture of old houses in Iron Gate shows Richard Keene's photographic gallery, at 24 Iron Gate, which is on the left with the glass roof. Twenty-four Iron Gate was the home from 1737, of John Whitehurst, the well-known horologer, scientist and philosopher. Born on 10 April 1713, he was the eldest son of John Whitehurst, a clock maker from Congleton. He was one of the foremost scientists of his day and a founder member of the Lunar Society. He became interested in geology while on long walks with his father in the Peak District. However, it was as a clock maker and engineer that Whitehurst is best known, his innovations included the round dial long case clock. The premises later served as a photographer's studio for Richard Keene who was born in London on 15 May 1825 and moved with his family to Derby three years later. After learning about printing, publishing and bookselling, he occupied the premises in Iron Gate where John Whitehurst had resided. It was not long before he developed an interest in photography, taking many scenes in Derby and Derbyshire. To provide a studio, the roof was removed and the present glass structure substituted. Photography dominated his business and he became known for high quality topographical views. At the time of his death in 1894, he had won 34 major awards, taken commissions from the Royal Family and was President Elect of the Photographic Convention of the United Kingdom.*

DMAG200537 - Picture courtesy of Derby Museums and Art Gallery

Crompton and Evans Bank and Iron Gate House c1910. *Iron Gate House was built by Samuel Crompton in the early 18th century; his father founded Derby's first bank in 1685. The ground floor was used as the family bank until 1880, when another bank, the Crompton and Evans Bank was built next door. In 1725, on the death of his father Samuel Junior took over the family's banking business, which provided him with sufficient capital to build the Friary, in Friar Gate. For a time he was the only financier in Derby. The notorious Heath Brothers only started money lending in 1745 and Thomas Evans in 1771. Samuel's son, another Samuel, succeeded him in 1757, both at the Friary and in banking. In the same year he became mayor of Derby, a position he held on two subsequent occasions a decade apart. The Heath Brothers went bankrupt in 1779 and the banks of both Evans and the Crompton family continued to thrive. Eventually both banks amalgamated and became the Crompton and Evans Union Bank, which was later absorbed by Nat West. Following a re-structuring programme the Nat West found they no longer had a need for the bank and it was converted into a public house, rather appropriately named the Standing Order. Iron Gate House is now occupied by the Thomas Leaper public house.*

Site of Joseph Wright's Birthplace, Iron Gate. *Joseph Wright was the third son of John Wright, attorney and town Clerk, and his wife Hannah Brooks. He was educated at Derby Free School in St Peter's Churchyard. During his teenage years he decided it was his vocation to become an artist, despite his father's disapproval. Today Wright is held in the highest regard both locally and internationally. There is an art gallery devoted to him in Derby Museum and Art Gallery; his paintings hang in the National Gallery, London, and in the Louvre, Paris. In 1997 an exhibition was put together with 260 of his paintings and drawings, celebrating the 200th anniversary of his death. The marble memorial pillar opposite Wright's birthplace depicts an Orrery, which is featured in one of his most famous works. The building in which he was born has been demolished.*

DMAG200506 - Picture courtesy of Derby Museums and Art Gallery

The George Inn. *The yard at the George Inn was used for theatrical performances in Elizabethan days. Notoriously, it was also the venue for cock fighting and a balconied extension was built so that patrons could watch that and other events. In 1850, a more praiseworthy event took place, when 12 carpenters meeting at the Bull's Head were told by a traveller about the 'Rochdale Pioneers'. They were founders of the Co-operative movement that aimed to create a society whose members would have an equal say in its running and who would benefit from its success. As a result of the meeting the Derby Co-operative Society was formed based on the £2 capital raised by the carpenters, who later became known as 'the Apostles'. They started the society by establishing a small store in a converted hay loft on the first floor of a stable block in the George Yard.*

Mr Jorrocks Public House (formerly the George Inn). *This picture was taken in August 1982, with a brewery horse drawn dray at the front of the pub, when it was re-opened following one of several name changes. It was built around 1648 and, during that era, was one of the most famous and busiest coaching inns in Derby. The London to Nottingham stage coach ran from 1735, and in 1766 the Post Office coach also ran from the inn. It had a wider frontage at that time, and in 1693, included the part now occupied by Foulds music shop. Alderman Samuel Heathcote, who re-fronted the building in 1693, was required by the Corporation to take out a 1,000 year lease on the 62 feet of frontage which pre 1936 encroached on the public thoroughfare. The original inn closed in 1853. The pub is now known simply as Jorrocks, the 'Mr' seen in the photograph havingy been dropped.*

DRBY005897 - Picture courtesy of Derby Evening Telegraph

CHAPTER 6 - DERBY CATHEDRAL QUARTER – TRAIL 2

Derby's first Market Charter was not particularly detailed, but the second, granted fifty years later, in 1204 by King John was much more precise. This Charter allowed a weekly market, held from Thursday to Friday evening and granted the Burgesses the right to levy tolls from the traders, as well as punish thieves. Later additions to the Charter gave the rights to hold fairs at Easter, Whitsun and Michaelmas.

In 2004, Derby celebrated the anniversary of two Royal Charters. The first marked the 850th anniversary of King Henry's Charter given to the Borough of Derby in 1154 and the second the 800th anniversary of King John's Charter, which was presented to Derby fifty years later.

The first Assembly Rooms to be built was in Full Street, and opened in 1714. The assemblies were conducted by Lady Patronesses drawn from notable local families and were very exclusive affairs. The building was soon deemed unsuitable, and the Duke of Devonshire provided a site for the new Assembly Rooms on the north side of the Market Place. Built in the mid 1700s, it became very popular with members of both sexes. It was unusual in that era for both men and women to attend public entertainment at the same time. There were strict rules on dress and single women had to be chaperoned.

Sadler Gate links Iron Gate with Bold Lane and The Strand and is a hive of activity during the day with the emphasis on shopping and eating. Evenings see a transformation, when the clubs, bars and pubs attract crowds of fun seekers and diners. The street has never been widened and has become much safer since pedestrianisation. In earlier days Sadler Gate had several busy coaching inns.

Assize Courts originated in the reign of Henry II, and were courts with a judge and jury. They sat with the authority of the monarch, bringing the King's Justice to the people. Initially, the assizes for both Derbyshire and Nottinghamshire were held in Nottingham. Until, in 1328, the Sheriff of Nottingham was instructed to provide suitable facilities in Derby.

The joint assizes were then held alternatively in Nottingham and Derby, until 1566, when separate assizes were held. In the mid 17th century, St Mary's Gate was selected as a suitable place to build a Shire Hall, which later became known as the County Hall. It was built by George Eaton of Etwall and competed in 1659. After that, St Mary's Gate was traditionally known as the legal quarter of Derby.

Derby Market Place. *A very detailed, 1894 picture of the Market Place, which almost certainly did not come into existence until around 1100 according to recent excavations. An ancient trackway used to run along the south side of where Derby Market Place now stands and was in existence many years before the town became part of the landscape. The Market Place was a focal point, both for trade and for social purposes, where shoppers and traders would exchange gossip as well as goods. It allowed producers to sell directly, and cut out profiteering middlemen as well as keeping prices down. Markets sprang up rapidly after the Norman Conquest. In the Cornmarket grain was traded; at the top end of Friar Gate farm animals were bought and sold along with produce. A market was also developed in the Morledge, where fairs were held. Until the 19th century, most of the market trading took place in the Old Market Square. This was much smaller than the present Market Place. The space was limited because on the west side were a group of buildings known as the Piazzas, and behind them, the Shambles. Despite the fact that the latter were filthy and rat invested, a number of butchers' shops still managed to do business.*

DMAG300195 - Picture courtesy of Derby Museums and Art Gallery

DRBY007787 - Picture courtesy of Derby City Council

Market stalls in the Market Place. *A busy day on the stalls as this c1912 picture depicts. The Market Place served several purposes; public meetings took place there, particularly at election time. It was also a place where criminals were exhibited and shamed. In 1757, a woman was whipped in public for pretending to be deaf and dumb in court. Fifteen years later, Thomas Bott, a farmer, sold his wife to a man from Langley Common for eighteen pence. He completed the deal by taking her to the purchaser at the Market Place with a halter round her waist. The market moved to the Morledge in 1933, and for a time the market place was used to park buses and cars. Now that through traffic has been removed it has been used as an event space. An ice skating rink has proved a very popular attraction, and the Big Wheel created quite a stir when it was first brought to Derby. But markets are not forgotten and regular monthly Farmers' Markets are still held, and specialty markets take place from time to time.*

Assembly Rooms. *A large part of the top side of the Market Place is taken up by the Assembly Rooms, which were built by Casson, Conder and Partners between 1973 and 1977. The building was designed to contain a large hall, small hall with bars and coffee shops separated by spacious foyers. Part of the elaborate plaster Jacobean ceiling from The Great Room of 18/19 Market Place was preserved and repositioned in the reception foyer outside the Darwin Suite. It was opened by the Queen Mother, with the opening concert performed by the Royal Philharmonic Orchestra.*

DRBY000835 - Picture courtesy of Derby Evening Telegraph

DRBY003009 - Picture courtesy of Derby City Council

The Former Assembly Rooms, Newcastle House. *The present Assembly Rooms have been preceded by two others, the first one was in Full Street, which opened in 1714. It was very exclusive and was conducted by Lady Patronesses drawn from notable local families, who ensured it remained so. However, it was rather small and not particularly striking and it was not long before it was not considered suitable for the assemblies. The building was later converted into a permanent theatre, which became known as the 'Little Theatre in Full Street'. The Duke of Devonshire provided a site for the new Assembly Rooms on the north side of the Market Place. They were built in 1752-5, but gutted by fire in 1963 and replaced. The stone façade of the previous Assembly Rooms was re-erected at Crich Tramway Museum, now renamed as Crich Tramway Village. The mid 1920s picture also shows H E Ramsden's Restaurant, which provided meals to those attending assemblies, and the Goose Boy Fountain.*

DRBY000773 - Picture courtesy of Derby City Council

Interior of the former Assembly Rooms. *An early 20th century picture of the magnificent interior of the former Assembly Rooms, which was one of Derby's very finest buildings. The Interior, shown here, was constructed in 1773-4. Robert and James Adam were asked in 1770 to submit designs for the interior. There is no evidence that they did so, but the ceiling was probably the work of Abraham Denstone, a plaster worker who had worked for Adam at Kedleston Hall. It was gutted by fire in 1963 and demolished. Part of the 17th century ceiling can still be seen in the foyer to the small hall at the new Darwin Suite.*

DMAG000033 - Picture courtesy of W W Winter

Franceys's Town House, Market Place. *Located on the Iron Gate side of the Market Place, Franceys's House particularly attracts the eye. It is one of Derby's most magnificent buildings, built c1694 for Alderman William Franceys, a well to do Alderman and apothecary. He was the only tradesman to be allowed to attend the very select County Assembly. An exception was made in his case, probably because he looked after the health of the county gentry. The house was an eight-bay, four storey dwelling with two massive reception rooms on the first floor, now divided. The frescoed ceilings were the work of Francis Bassano.*

DRBY004699 - Picture courtesy of Derby City Council

Iron Gate and Sadler Gate Corner. *This c1900 picture of Iron Gate and Sadler Gate Corner, used to be something of an accident 'black spot.' It was a main road in medieval times, but no longer do coaches try to turn the corner at breakneck speed. In May 1837, a lady was knocked down and suffered a broken leg on the corner as she tried to get out of the way of a carriage. Two years later, a coach with four horses failed to navigate the corner and crashed into the wall. There were also other minor mishaps and near misses. The house on the top side of the corner was probably built by Roger Morledge, about 1695 for Alderman Joshua Smith. It later became Bemrose's shop, before eventually being taken over by Lloyd's Bank, who removed the roof, replacing, it with a flat one.*

DRBY004378 - Picture courtesy of Derby City Council

Top: Sadler Gate late 1800s.

Sadler Gate, unlike Iron Gate, has not been widened and is now virtually traffic free. It probably originated as a route to the Wardwick and Ashbourne Road beyond, when the market place began its development c1100. The name indicates that it was an area where saddlery businesses had been set up in ancient days. The street is much older than it appears on casual examination, the fronts of the buildings have been modernised to keep up with fashion giving the viewer a false impression. However, the rears of the buildings have been left untouched. A walk along the various yards soon reveals many of the properties date back to the 17th century. In particular, George Yard, a long narrow thoroughfare that runs parallel to Sadler Gate, exposes many of the secrets as to the age of the properties.

Bottom: Sadler Gate 1923.

DMAG300031 - Picture courtesy of Derby Museums and Art Gallery

DMAG300034 - Picture courtesy of Derby Museums and Art Gallery

The Bell Hotel - Sadler Gate. *In earlier days Sadler Gate had several busy coaching inns. Minimal time was allowed for passengers to seek refreshment and for horses to be changed, before the coachman's horn sounded for departure. The Bell still survives from that era, the 1922 picture showing the building before the new front was added by Ford and Weston as part of a decorative refurbishment in 1929 using black and white mock-Tudor timbering rescued from other local sites. It was the Meynell family who built this splendid old coaching inn around 1680. John Campion acquired the freehold in 1780. During the floods of 1842, the nine year old grandson of John Campion II was 'launched in a wash-tub in the cellars' - the purpose to save some vintage bottles of wine placed there by his great-grandfather! The Bell was a favourite watering-hole for local politicians, some of whom tried to bribe the local electorate to vote for them by providing free drinks on Polling Day. Sir Henry Harpur in his quest to get elected even had a list of 42 public houses, including The Bell, where voters benefited from his bribe at election time. Those who did not have the right to vote tended to riot in disappointment both at missing out on the ballot and also the free beer!*

DRBY005153 - Picture courtesy of Derby Evening Telegraph

Blacksmith's Yard, Sadler Gate

This is a 1980s picture of the Old Blacksmith's Yard, which is a particularly attractive courtyard off Sadler Gate. As the name implies it was a blacksmith's yard where horses were once shod. However, it has been used for many other purposes and was known as Palfree's Yard, following the occupation of Samuel Palfree in the late 1800s. His granddaughter, Barbara Mary Palfree, a vetinerary surgeon, had an animal hospital there until 1979. The yard was then redeveloped by David Adams and a modified version of the 15th century merchant's house, found behind the former Assembly Rooms, when the new building was under construction, was rebuilt in the yard.

DMAG200233 - Picture courtesy of Derby Museums and Art Gallery

Sadler Gate from Sadler Gate Bridge. *It may seem a little strange to the visitor walking down Sadler Gate to see a sign at the bottom of the street, above a shop indicating 'Sadler Gate Bridge'. The bridge rebuilt by William Strutt in 1786 is now covered over following the culverting of Markeaton Brook in the late 1800s. This enabled a new street, called the Strand to be formed. Originally the bridge gave access across Markeaton Brook to Cheapside and beyond. The picture dates from 1913 and shows Mason's Oil and Colour corner shop on the right.*

St Werburgh's Church, Cheapside. *The former settlement of Wardwick has had a church at its centre since at least 700AD. St Werburgh's Church, on the corner of Cheapside and Friar Gate has been re-built many times. Its medieval steeple collapsed in 1601 and the remainder of its fabric in 1658. The main problem being the frequency with which the Markeaton Brook flooded, a problem not resolved until after the floods of 1932, when finally remedial action was taken. The oldest part of the church still in existence is the tower of 1601. This 1880s view of St Werburgh's Church, shows the Hansom Cab rank, which stood with the cabbie's shelter on the right. Patented in 1834 by the English architect Joseph Hansom, this type of vehicle quickly gained acceptance as a public cab. It was redesigned a number of times, with the innovation of putting the driver high up behind the cab probably the most significant change. The cab to the rear of the queue in the picture is a Hansom cab.*

DRBY001242 - Picture courtesy of Derby City Council

DRBY001739 - Picture courtesy of Derby City Council

The interior of St Werburgh's Church. *The interior of St Werburgh's Church, in 1891, which shows the altar, before the installation of the mosaic images in the reredos in 1898. The Church, closed for worship in the 1980s, later opening as a shopping gallery, but this venture was not a success and it closed down after a few years. It re-opened recently as a Chinese restaurant, but that too only lasted for a short period before closing its doors. A Trust cares for the tower and the old chancel. The tower was built in the Gothic Survival style between 1601/8, and the chancel of 1690 retains much of its contemporary woodwork and furnishings, including a superb iron font cover by Robert Bakewell. The fine reredos dates to 1708 and was designed by Henry Huss. The register dates back to 1588 and it was here that Doctor Johnson, the creator of the English Dictionary, married Elizabeth 'Tetty' Porter on the 7 July 1735. It is thought that the marks on the exterior walls were made by cannonballs during the Civil War.*

DRBY007574 - Picture courtesy of Derby City Council

Derby Gas Light Company and Gas showrooms, Friar Gate. *Friar Gate is one of Derby's most ancient streets, and has retained many of its older buildings. The former Derby Gas, Light and Coke Company showrooms and offices used to operate from the premises, pictured in 1970. Built in 1889, the name of the company can still be seen on the wall of this fine Victorian building. The first public gas lamp was lit in the Market Place, on 19 February 1821. Twenty years later, an Act of Parliament allowed Derby Gas Light and Coke Company to supply customers outside the Borough, leading to further expansion. In the 1960s the building was converted to a shop for British Gas with large plate-glass windows installed to make it look more like a modern shop. It was the first steel framed building in Derby and is now Grade II listed.*

Gell's House, Friar Gate. *Gell's House is Derby's finest surviving complete 17th century town house. The four storey gabled building was the Parliamentary head quarters during the English Civil war. It was probably built for Col Thomas Gell, the brother of Sir John Gell the notorious governor of Derby during the war. The Gell family lived at Hopton Hall for nearly 500 years and were the dominating influence in the area before it was sold in 1989. The Hall hides behind a red brick crinkle-crankle wall on the eastern side of Hopton. The wall traps the rays of the sun to assist fruit growing. The 1921 picture which looks down Friar Gate, also shows the entrance gates to the Friary, in the right foreground.*

DMAG200173 - Picture courtesy of Derby Museums and Art Gallery

The Friary Hotel, Friar Gate. *The Friary Hotel was built on part of the grounds that once belonged to a Dominican Monastery. Here a large friary was erected with approximately 16 acres of parkland featuring fishponds, a chapel and other buildings. In 1731, Samuel Crompton built a fine townhouse on the site where The Friary Hotel, a Grade II * listed building now stands. On his father's death in 1725, Samuel Junior had taken over the family's banking business and this provided him with the capital to build the Friary. It was extended in 1760, 1875 and in the 1950s. The Boden family lived there from 1873 to 1922. Henry Boden and his wife Mary worked tirelessly for temperance, but following the death of her husband, in 1922, his widow sold the house to the Whitaker family. Shortly afterwards they set about transforming it into a licensed hotel, much to the infuriation of Mrs Boden. The c1869 picture shows a group of ladies playing croquet in the garden.*

Joseph Wright Centre. *The £12m Joseph Wright Centre facility is part of Derby College and follows the merger of Mackworth, Broomfield and Wilmorton Colleges. The name originates from the internationally famous, local artist whose work in the mid to late 18th Century was inspired by scientific and technological art forms. The building's high-impact design produced by local architects is unique to Derby and covers 6,600 square meters of floor space over four storeys. As a result of the success of the centre over the first two years, the building has been extended to increase study and social space for students.*

DRBY004437 - Picture courtesy of Derby Evening Telegraph

The Theatre Royal - Gospel Hall, Bold Lane. *The Royal Theatre, as it was originally called, pictured in 1937. Built in 1773, and paid for by James Whiteley, was opened on 13 September of that year. It was converted from a malthouse, which had been built about 60 years previously. The first play performed at the theatre was Oliver Goldsmith's 'She stoops to conquer.' Famous actors came up from London to perform for short seasons. It closed in 1864, possibly because it was too small, and was sold to William Wilkins, and re-opened as a Gospel Hall. When this re-located after the Second World War, it became a library and then a Magistrates' Court, which closed in 2003. It is now a restaurant.*

County Hall (Crown Court), St Mary's Gate. *The Shire Hall, later known as the County Hall, was designed by George Eaton of Etwall and completed in 1659. Originally it was used for concerts, plays, and gatherings, as well as courts and assizes. This ended in 1714, when the new Assembly Rooms were built. The buildings then became exclusively a Crown Court, with an inn added on one side around 1795 and Judges' Lodgings on the other side in 1811. The courts closed in 1989 and moved to the Morledge and, after going into decline for a number of years, have been superbly renovated and converted into the city's Magistrates' Court. This c1827 view is an engraving by Orlando Jewitt, who was a self-taught wood engraver.*

DRBY004383 - Picture courtesy of Derby City Council

DRBY000915 - Picture courtesy of Derby Evening Telegraph

County Hall, St Mary's Gate. *In this picture, probably taken in the 1930s, the Mayoral coach and attendants are seen standing in the courtyard of County Hall. Its main function was to hold the Assizes and retain the prisoners during trials. The first day of the Assize was always a colourful occasion, when following attending an Assizes service at All Saints' Church (now Derby Cathedral), the Judges arrived by coach in the Courtyard. They were preceded by halberdiers and trumpeters, whose trumpets bore the banners of the High Sheriff of the year. The enclosed courtyard set out with stone gate piers and iron railings flanked by the late Georgian buildings is a notable feature long admired by the passing public. The Kings' Arms County Hotel was built on the left hand side of the building to provide convenient lodging for plaintiffs, defendants, supporters and lawyers and just over ten years later the Judges' Lodgings were added opposite the hotel. The Dukes of Devonshire also used the Judge's Lodgings as their Derby residence.*

All Saints Church and St Mary's Gate. *This postcard was published in the first series of Derby Ram postcards in 1903, looking up St Mary's Gate towards what is now the Cathedral. The shadow of the Baptist Chapel can be seen on the gable of a house on the left. The chapel was once St Mary's Gate House, built for the Osbourne Family, but later sold to the General Baptists for conversion into a chapel and now demolished. The Cathedral Quarter Hotel now occupies the building on the extreme left of the picture. It was Derby's first boutique hotel, opened by Finesse Hotels early in 2008.*

DMAG000678 - Picture courtesy of Richard Keene Ltd

CHAPTER 7 - DERBY CATHEDRAL QUARTER – TRAIL 3

The Guildhall Theatre, owned by Derby City Council, holds a number of concerts, plays and recitals. On the ground floor a regular programme of exhibitions takes place. Along with the Assembly Rooms, the Guildhall has hosted the CAMRA Real Ale Beer Festival. The Round House hosted the winter 2012 festival. Derby is the Real Ale capital of England since its foundation in 1971; CAMRA has been extremely successful in promoting quality, choice and value for money and preventing the takeover of small breweries. No new ale breweries were set up in the UK for the 50 years before CAMRA was founded. There are now around 300 new brewers producing real ale, forming part of a massive real ale revival.

The Athenaeum Society, which had been established to supervise the culverting of the Markeaton Brook, also drew up plans to re-develop the corner site of the Cornmarket and Victoria Street. At the time a good quality hotel in the centre of the town was a prime requirement. This was recognised by the society and plans were drawn up and the Royal Hotel was built in 1837.

The idea of a Mechanics Institute first emerged in Scotland at the end of the 18th century, where at the University of Glasgow, two professors, John Anderson and George Birkbeck began offering free lectures to the working people of Glasgow. When Anderson died in 1796 he left all his money to found Anderson's College. Birkbeck worked as professor of natural philosophy at the college, but eventually moved to London where he founded the London Mechanics Institute. Between 1820 and 1860, Mechanics' Institutes became a common sight in most towns in Britain and the United States for the voluntary education of skilled manual workers. They were often funded by wealthy local industrialists.

An increasing number of people now visit Derby Museum and Art Gallery with the express intention of viewing Joseph Wright's work. His popularity has grown in recent years and he is today recognised internationally as a major artist of the 18th century. Although Derby Museum contains the best collection of his work anywhere, not all his pictures are likely to be on show at one time as paintings are often lent to support exhibitions at other galleries. Many of his paintings have also been bought by people living in the United States.

Derby's first Town Hall, Market Place. *The painting is a sepia water colour and was probably painted after c1900. It is a somewhat imaginary scene which may have been based on an earlier drawing or painting. The picture shows the Old Town Hall building; a late medieval jettied timber-framed structure which stood in the Market Place and which was replaced by the Town Hall, or Guildhall, as it is more usually referred to nowadays.*

DRBY005433 - Picture courtesy of Derby Museum and Art Gallery

Derby Town Hall – Guildhall, Market Place. *This photograph was taken by H A Wallace in the early 1900s of a drawing by Alfred John Keene. The painting was originally a water colour, with somewhat imaginary scenery, which may have been based on an earlier drawing or painting. The picture shows the New Town Hall (Guildhall) building in 1839. The Guildhall was built in 1828 by Habershon, but was later remodelled after a fire in 1841-2 by Duesbury and Lee. They gave the Guildhall its central tower and domical cap which is not shown in this picture. There was a labyrinth of tunnels and catacombs that ran under the Guildhall. In Victorian times they were used to take prisoners from the old Police Station in Lock-Up Yard to the Assizes that were held in the Guildhall. One of the best remembered to be escorted through the tunnels was Alice Wheeldon, a left wing revolutionary, from Peartree in Derby. She was the key individual involved in a plot to assassinate the Prime Minister, Lloyd George, in 1917. Wheeldon was captured and tried at the Assize Court and given a ten year sentence, while her co-conspirators got lesser terms.*

DRBY003232 - Picture courtesy of Derby City Council

The Guildhall and Market Place 19th century

The Guildhall was built in 1730 on the site of the previous hall. The 1825 Derby Improvement Act required it to be rebuilt and the new Guildhall (pictured) was built in 1828. It was designed by Matthew Habershon and built at a cost of £7,000 in a Grecian style, and contained the Court of Sessions. On 21 October 1841 it burnt down, leaving only the outside walls. Henry Duesbury was commissioned to design a replacement. This 19th century illustration is captioned 'Town Hall June 28'. It shows Druids leading a procession of townsfolk from the Market Place to the Arboretum for its opening. The former Council Chamber with its elaborately plastered ceiling is now occupied by a small theatre.

The Guildhall and Market Place c1905

In this picture of the Guildhall and Market Place, the Shot Tower can be seen peeping up behind the Guildhall to the left, and the Derbyshire Advertiser building on the right. Further to the left is the junction with Tennant Street. The statue, front right, is of Michael Thomas Bass MP and benefactor to Derby, sympathetic to workers and Trade Unions, and who refused all offers of Baronetcy and Peerage. The statue is now located in Museum Square. Note the Hansom cabman's shelter beyond the market stalls in the foreground, and the line of Hansom Cabs.

DRBY006480 - Picture courtesy of Derby City Council

War Memorial, Market Place. *Airmen laying wreaths on 15 October 1980 to mark the fortieth anniversary of the Battle of Britain air battle. The War Memorial is made up of bronze figures on a stone plinth with a stone background cross. It was unveiled on the 11 November 1924, by Alderman Oswald Ling, and repositioned, in 1994, as part of the Derby Promenade street improvement works. Charles Clayton Thompson was the memorial's designer and A G Walker, ARA, was responsible for the carving. The Assembly Rooms are clearly in view in the background.*

DRBY000394 - Picture courtesy of Derby Evening Telegraph

Waterfall, Market Place - Well Dressing commemorating Joseph Wright. *In an area reserved for relaxation, where visitors can sit and rest, The Waterfall provides a most unusual feature. It was constructed as part of the City Council, 'Derby Promenade', a scheme that stretched from the Spot to the Cathedral, involving pedestrianisation of the route. The Waterfall came in for a lot of criticism, but not from the younger generation who love it, particularly when the weather is warm and the sun is shining. It has also provided a reason for an annual Well Dressing to be started in Derby, which seems fitting in a county where 'Well Dressing' still flourishes so strongly. The Well Dressing in the picture commemorates Joseph Wright the famous artist, who was born in Iron Gate, Derby, in 1734.*

DRBY003043 - Picture courtesy of Eric Matthews

DRBY004079 - Picture courtesy of Derby City Council

Market Hall interior - during construction. *The covered Market Hall hides behind the Guildhall and is one of Derby's greatest treasures. It is a fine example of Victorian architecture with a spectacular vaulted roof, using iron supplied by a nearby foundry. Inside, there is a wealth of unusual, classic and traditional stalls, shops and café bars. It cost £29,000 to build, and was officially opened on 29 May 1866, by the Mayor, Frederick Longdon. At the opening ceremony the Duke of Devonshire gave a speech and there were parades through the town. A choir of 600 performed the 'Messiah'. At that time the hall contained 38 butchers' shops and 150 stalls, which sold flowers, fruit, vegetables, books, newspapers, grocery, jewellery, sewing machines, sweets and toys. On the balcony there were refreshments stalls and a number of drapers. One problem was that when the weather was wintry both traders and shoppers felt bitterly cold as the Market Hall had no doors. However, following a deputation from the stall holders the markets committee agreed to fit doors.*

Derby Market Hall. *The Market Hall pictured in 1866, the year it was opened to the public. Over the years it has adapted to changing circumstances and there has been a growth of service stalls. The Fish Market left the Market Place in 1926 and was re-located on the south side of the Market Hall. In an annexe there is a Poultry Market. The interior of the Market Hall was completely refurbished in 1938, resulting in the elegant balcony being boarded up. In July 1987, the Market Hall was closed for major repairs and renovation. The objectives were modernisation and the need to return it to its original appearance as a Victorian listed building. It was reopened by HRH Princess Margaret in 1989, and is the home to many long established traders.*

DRBY005453 - Picture courtesy of Derby City Council

DRBY005457 - Picture courtesy of Derby Museum and Art Gallery

Rear of Market Hall, 1970 (top) and 1985 (bottom). *Today when you leave the Market Hall by the doors at the southern end you reach Osnabruck Square, named after Derby's twin city in Germany. A stone pillar in the centre of the square announces that the German city is 500 miles away. Osnabruck was founded in 780AD, and has many historic buildings and, like Derby, is close to beautiful countryside. As a result of the twinning arrangements many events and activities have taken place connecting the two cities. Formerly this was the site of Strutt's Calico factory and the former fish market. The fish market that once stood in the square was demolished in 1981, and re-sited in the Lockup Yard off the Cornmarket. The picture at the top, taken in 1970, shows the Market Hall and the Fish Market before it was removed. The picture below, was taken 15 years later and again shows the Market Hall, but the Fish Market has gone and been replaced by Osnabruck Square.*

DRBY002949 - Picture courtesy of Derby Evening Telegraph

DRBY003241 - Picture courtesy of Derby City Council

Corn Exchange, Albert Street. *Following long standing complaints that corn dealers were obstructing the footpaths in the Cornmarket, the Corn Exchange was built in 1861, opening the next year. It became the Palace Theatre of Varieties in 1897 and 22 years later the Palais de Danse. Dancing was advertised 'twice nightly', but this was not strictly correct as the first session started at 3pm at a cost of 1s 6d and the second at 7.30pm costing 2s 6d. Friday was a special night, where those present had to pay 5s with evening dress compulsory. In 1914, the dance hall closed on the outbreak of war and in 1919, it became Palais de Danse. The Corn Exchange contained luxurious lounges, tea and supper rooms until the Derby Evening Telegraph took it over for offices in 1929.*

Corn Exchange Fine Arts Exhibition.

DRBY002924 - Picture courtesy of Derby City Council

DCHQ502929 - Picture courtesy of A P Knighton

Albert Street. *Albert Street was named after HRH Prince Albert and came into existence when Markeaton Brook was culverted. The former Trent Bus Station, with its panelled roof and triangular infill, is on the left facing the Corn Exchange. After nearly 50 years of costly circulation wars the Derby Telegraph merged with its rival, The Express, on the 29 January 1932. The Express was owned by Allied Northern Newspapers, and Northcliffe Newspapers owned the Derby Telegraph. The two papers were combined and the joint paper was published at Northcliffe House, the new name given to the Corn Exchange. As new technology was introduced, it became obvious the building was too small to accommodate all the equipment and the move to new premises, on the banks of the River Derwent, began at the end of 1979.*

Debenham's, Victoria Street. *This picture was taken on 24 November 1982, showing Debenham's Departmental Store with its interesting curved shaped frontage, which it occupied prior to moving to the Westfield in 2007. Before Debenham's, Ranby's Departmental Store traded from the site. Victoria Street starts and Albert Street ends at the intersection between the Cornmarket and St Peter's Street. It was named after Queen Victoria and like its neighbour came into being as a result of the culverting of the Markeaton Brook.*

DRBY006263 - Picture courtesy of Derby Evening Telegraph

DMAG001632 - Picture courtesy of Derby Museums and Art Gallery

Outside Ranby's, Victoria Street. *This c1950 view is believed to show a Derby Corporation Omnibus Department outing to New Brighton. The coach has been hired from Barton's, and is parked outside Ranby's Department Store. Woolworth's (in the background) moved to the new Eagle Centre in the mid-1970s. Sadly, all the Woolworth Stores in the country closed down as a result of the recession in the 21st century. They had become something of a national institution, closing after 99 years trading. The Omnibus Department Offices were in a building, which originally opened in 1904 as Tramway offices. Once the department took over, the shop on the street level was used as an enquiry office and crew room. The building is now the Post Office.*

The Royal Hotel, Cornmarket. *The Royal Hotel, pictured in 1905, on the corner of the Cornmarket and Victoria Street was built in 1837 by Robert Wallace, after he won a competition to design it. In total 52 architects' submitted proposals, from which Wallace was chosen, to design a group of buildings, originally consisting of a hotel, the Athenaeum and a Post Office. He had also been selected to design the Derby and Derbyshire Bank, which was adjacent to the proposed new development, which meant he could easily merge the two developments. The Athenaeum Society premises faced Victoria Street; it was the home to a news room where the latest editions of some 18 different newspapers and journals were available for members to study. It also housed the new Town and Country Museum.*

DRBY001261 - Picture courtesy of Derby City Council

DRBY001060 - Picture courtesy of Derby City Council

Royal Hotel, Cornmarket - Queen Victoria's Royal Visit Procession. *The picture shows Burton Band, in front of the Royal Hotel for Queen Victoria's visit to Derby, on the 21 May 1891. She laid the foundation stone at Derby General Infirmary, which was then called the Derbyshire Royal Infirmary. Queen Victoria also knighted Derby Mayor and MP, Alfred Haslam at Derby Railway Station. He had paid out of his own pocket for the lavish welcoming displays all along the route of the Royal visit. Built in 1837, the Royal Hotel soon became the most popular place to stay for visitors as well as for local celebrations.*

The Great Flood, Cornmarket. *This is a view of the Cornmarket during the floods of September 1931, with a lone boatman paddling his way along the middle of the street. The flood was caused when the Markeaton Brook culvert which runs through the centre of the city overflowed. Having had to put up with Derby's worst floods for 50 years in 1931, the floods the following year were even worse. The damage was estimated at £400,000 and the Mayor launched a relief fund.*

DMAG200302 - Picture courtesy of Derby Museums and Art Gallery

DRBY006607 - Picture courtesy of Derby Evening Telegraph

Top picture - Cornmarket, c1910

Cornmarket

The Cornmarket is noticeably wider at the bottom end which faces St Peter's Street. The Normans in 1100 had brought over the idea of street markets. However one general market that provided for all requirements did not work and it was soon realised that markets had to be divided up into special categories. Corn merchants, for example, needed to be set apart from the beast market so that their produce would not be eaten. This led to the bottom end of the Cornmarket being deliberately constructed so that it was wider than the rest and therefore able to accommodate the Grain Markets. Merchants placed samples of grain in containers sited on posts so that potential buyers could test them before purchase. The market continued to operate in the Cornmarket, until the Corn Exchange was built on Albert Street. Both the photographs on this page show busy Cornmarket scenes with trams, hansom cabs and, in the lower of the two pictures, a man pulling a Stead & Simpson advertising hoarding, mounted on a hand cart. He is outside Salmon & Gluckstein's tobacconist shop, which proclaimed that they were the 'largest and the cheapest tobacconist in the world'.

Bottom picture - Cornmarket, 1906

DMAG000323 - Picture courtesy of Derby Museums and Art Gallery

Entrance to Lock up yard, Cornmarket. *Pictured in the 1980s, it was once the scene of the brutal murder of a policeman. On the 12 July 1879, Gerald Mainwaring, after drinking heavily, set off driving a horse and trap through the streets of Derby. He was accompanied by a prostitute, Annie Green, and with Mainwaring flogging the pony and both occupants laughing and shouting at passersby, the police at first tried and failed to check their progress. Eventually the pair were apprehended in the yard of the Traveller's Rest on Ashbourne Road. They were taken back to the police station in Lock-up Yard, where they were charged with being drunk and disorderly. Unfortunately they were not searched and when Annie Green took exception to being locked up and hit one of the policemen on the jaw, the officers moved to restrain her. At that point Mainwaring produced a pistol and shot PC Moss, who subsequently died; he also shot at and injured another officer. Mainwaring was sentenced to be hanged, but the decision was made on the toss of a coin by the foreman after the jury had been unable to reach a verdict. This came to the notice of the local paper and the editor contacted the Home Secretary who commuted the sentence to life imprisonment, ruling that a man should not be hanged based on the toss of a coin.*

DRBY006609 - Picture courtesy of Derby Evening Telegraph

The unveiling of the Steve Bloomer Memorial, Lock up Yard. *The memorial to Steve Bloomer was unveiled on 28 October 1996, and reads: STEVE BLOOMER 'The first king of English football goalscorers, entered the 20th century with his fame as Derby County's outstanding marksman already established. As the next century beckoned – this monument was erected in 1996 – his Rams' all games record of 332 goals was still unsurpassed. His 353 Football League goals for Derby County and Middlesbrough was a record until near his death in 1938 at 64. Bloomer's 28 goals in 23 England games gave him a then unique average of 1.21 per cap. The son of a Midlands' blacksmith, Bloomer was a pupil at St James' School in Derby.'*

DRBY001268 - Picture courtesy of Derby City Council

DRBY000321 - Picture courtesy of Derby Evening Telegraph

The Tiger Bar, Lock-up Yard, off Cornmarket. *Opposite St James Street, in the Lock-up Yard, is the Tiger public house. It dates from 1737, when it operated as a coaching inn, and was originally much larger. It was used by travellers between London and Manchester, when the frontage stretched as far as the Cornmarket. The building was restored in 1990. It is a popular stopping place for parties on ghost walks. As the Tiger Bar provides access for a subterranean trip down into the barrel-vaulted tunnels beneath the Guild Hall, in search of ghosts. The picture was taken in 1991.*

The end of St James' Lane and Bridge. *This c 1850s picture shows the end of St James' Lane, before Markeaton Brook was culverted to create the Strand. St James' Street was formerly known as St James' Lane. It was described in the 1860s as a narrow, unsightly and unsavoury alley, before it was widened. The work was paid for by the building of St James' Hotel. After completion it was renamed St James' Street and became an elegant shopping thoroughfare. In February 1957, a mini earthquake hit Derby, buildings started to shake and walls, ceilings and floors shivered and shook. People frightened by the commotion ran into the streets. St James' Street had to be closed so that heavy coping stones, each weighing about two hundred pounds, that had been dislodged, could be made safe.*

DMAG002068 - Picture courtesy of Derby Museums and Art Gallery

DRBY007895 - Picture courtesy of Derby City Council

The Wardwick, showing the Mechanics' Institute. *Although the spelling has changed, it is one of Derby's oldest street names and is recorded in 1085 as Walwick Strete. It was close to the Wardwick that the Mercians first established a village settlement quite distinct and apart from the later Saxon settlement of Derby. A small church dedicated to St Werburgh was built around 700 AD, but it was sited too close to the brook and its foundations became unsafe due to flooding. The picture dates from around 1900.*

Presentation Derby Mechanics' Institute, Wardwick. *The presentation in this 1952 picture is being made by Mr S Laughton at the Mechanics' Institute. There were classes for reading, writing, arithmetic, drawing, music, French and chemistry. A class also met weekly to discuss literary and scientific subjects. The library contained nearly 6,000 volumes and newspapers and periodicals were provided. The premises were open from early in the morning until ten at night. The institute had a number of famous visitors including, Charles Dickens the author and actor and Franz Liszt, the Hungarian born pianist and composer.*

DRBY007767 - Picture courtesy of Derby City Council

DRBY004309 - Picture courtesy of Lu Vernon

Flood Marker, Wardwick. *An iron plaque is fixed to the front of the Wardwick Tavern that marks the level the flood waters reached on 1 April 1842; subsequent rises in the level of the street reduces the true impact of the sign. The flood was caused by Markeaton Brook bursting its banks in the days when it flowed on the surface through the town centre. This was exceeded by a similar flood on the 22 May 1932, when the brook burst its culvert, causing considerable loss of stock to businesses in the vicinity that used their cellars for storage.*

Wardwick Tavern. *The Wardwick Tavern is a well proportioned three storey inn, built in 1708 for the Alsop family, although parts of an earlier stone building still remain. After the Alsop's sold the pub, it was purchased by the Lowes', a well known brewing family, who built a brewery at the rear. This was considerably enlarged by the Alton family when they came into ownership. In the 1930s the brewery buildings were demolished to make way for a Telephone Exchange, which itself was replaced 40 years later. The remaining premises were used until the late 1960s as brewery offices, when in 1969; Allied Breweries opened their redundant offices as a pub.*

DMAG300017 - Picture courtesy of Derby Museums and Art Gallery

Wardwick - before widening. *This picture was taken around the turn of the 20th century, before the road was widened in 1914. As a result of the demolition three large houses on the north side of the road were pulled down. In addition a garden was created by the museum, an extension of which in 1984 created the present Museum Square. The iron railings and gates were re-erected in front of the park facing Nightingale Road. At roughly the same time that the road was widened, the Museum and Art Gallery were expanded.*

The Library and Museum, Wardwick. *This is a pre-1905 picture of Derby Library and Museum on the Wardwick, which was built in 1876-1879 to a competition winning design by R K Freeman of Bolton in a Gothic design with a Franco-Flemish tower and Arts-and-Crafts detailing, including wrought iron by Edwin Haslam around a frescoed gallery. The foundation stone was laid by Michael Thomas Bass, a member of the Burton brewing company, an MP for Derby and a benefactor of the town who paid for its construction. The Museum and Art Gallery were expanded in 1915, and again in 1965, when T W East added the Modernist-style building facing the Strand. In the picture some road repairs are taking place in the foreground, at the junction with Becket Street.*

DMAG000232 - Picture courtesy of Derby Museums and Art Gallery

DRBY003214 - Picture courtesy of Derby City Council

Right: Bass Statue in Museum Square, 1969. *Derby Museum and Art Gallery run a programme of special exhibitions supporting permanent displays relating to the city's archaeology, history, wildlife and local regiments. The new Ceramics Gallery provides an additional attraction. The Bonnie Prince Charlie Room commemorates the important role played by Derby in the Jacobite Uprising of 1745. There are special geology and wildlife features, with a Time Tunnel, walk-in cave, hands-on exhibits and a series of authentic looking Derbyshire wildlife settings. The Joseph Wright Art Gallery attracts a large number of visitors.*

Below: Derby Museum and Art Gallery 1970

DRBY005429 - Picture courtesy of Derby Museum and Art Gallery

DMAG200150 - Picture courtesy of Derby Museums and Art Gallery

Jacobean House from the garden, 1894. *The finest Jacobean House in Derby, it was most probably built in 1611, in the Wardwick. Once much larger, having five gables, until in 1855, it was sympathetically reduced in size by architect John Price, to make way for Becket Street. It is still a magnificent decorative building, despite being much diminished in both size and splendour following its partial demolition. It was for many years the home of the Gisborne family and the grounds extended to two acres. It was built of red brick for the Gisborne family, making it the first brick building to be built in Derby. The Heathcote and Jessop families also used it as a town house. In recent years it has served various commercial purposes including an estate agents' office and café bar. The ground floor windows were lowered in 1960. In the picture below, the corner of the Mundy House can be seen.*

Jacobean House, 1981

DRBY002045 - Picture courtesy of Derby Evening Telegraph

DRBY004731 - Picture courtesy of Derby City Council

The Strand. *The Strand came into existence when the decision was made to culvert Markeaton Brook from Sadler Gate Bridge to St James' Bridge, forming a new street in the process. Sir Abraham Woodiwiss, who was Mayor of Derby from 1880-82, built the Strand including the Strand Arcade and parts of St James's Street in 1878-81 as a commercial venture. The architects were Giles and Brookhouse, except for the Arcade, which was designed by John Story. The foundation stone was laid by Alderman Sir Henry Bemrose on 30 September 1878. The great curve of the building frontages, the balustrade entrances, the highly decorated stonework and neatly arranged windows gives a real feeling of anticipation and interest to the visitor walking along the street. Named after the Strand in London, it is pictured here in 1939. The entrance to the museum and shop is at the Bold Lane end of the street. The shop sells a range of souvenirs, slides, postcards and books on local topics.*

DRBY006597 - Picture courtesy of Derby Evening Telegraph

Strand Arcade. *The Victorian Strand Arcade, pictured in 1985, was created in the early 1870s. It was fashioned in 'debased classical style'; to replicate London's Burlington Arcade from designs by John Story and built in 1880. The Strand Arcade links Sadler Gate and the Strand, and has been described as 'a unique link between different ages and city cultures'. Sadler Gate dating from medieval times winds its way from Iron Gate to Bold Lane in an informal, jumbled fashion. This contrasts with the formal appearance of the Strand Arcade, with its tall and impressive stone, three-storey entrance off Sadler Gate. The exit into the Strand is equally agreeable.*

CHAPTER 8 - ALLESTREE, MARKEATON AND MACKWORTH

ALLESTREE

Allestree, a pleasant residential suburb on the northern periphery of Derby, has its own shopping centre at Park Farm and is the home of Derby University. It is almost surrounded by agricultural land and attractive parks. Markeaton Park is to the south, Allestree Park on the north and Darley Abbey Park on the eastern side; only a short distance away to the southwest, set in beautiful parkland of its own, is Kedleston Hall.

The Anglo-Saxons settled at Allestree, no doubt attracted by its good southerly facing location, the quality of the soil and most of all the plentiful supply of water. However, it is unlikely that they were the first people to settle, at least temporarily in the area, as a barbed and tanged arrowhead, dating back to the Bronze Age, was found in a garden at Allestree in the 1970s.

Prior to the Norman Conquest, Allestree was nothing more than a tiny hamlet of scattered dwellings, part of the holding of the Earl of Northumbria. For years the village was almost completely self sufficient with the villagers having to rely on their own efforts to feed, cloth and shelter themselves and their children.

After the Norman invasion, it was recorded in the Domesday Book of 1086, as a berewick, or outlier of the Manor of Markeaton held by the Earl of Chester. The Earl's Steward, Jocelyn, an ancestor of the Touchet family of Markeaton, who later succeeded to the manor, controlled the estate. In the middle of the 12th century most of the land was granted and sold to the recently founded Abbey of St Mary at Darley, and then much of it rented back to the Touchet family.

In 1516, the manor of Markeaton, which included Allestree, came into the hands of John Mundy, a goldsmith, who six years later became the Lord Mayor of London. The Mundy family were anxious to make the most of their acquisition and with the final break up of the feudal system of farming, innovative methods were experimented with to improve stock raising and crop production. These new initiatives and the expansion of trade as the country moved into another era, gradually led to improvements in the standard of living of the villagers.

The estate remained in the hands of the Mundy family until the 1780s, when Francis Noel Clarke Mundy, sold most of it, but retained the title of lord of the manor. By the middle of the next century, a large number of Allestree's residents were employed at the Darley Abbey cotton mills.

Trail: Allestree Park – St Edmund's Close – Cornhill – Duffield Road – Ford Lane.

Allestree Hall - hall and gardens. *Bache Thornhill of Stanton-in-Peak bought and enclosed Allestree Park and commenced the building of a hall in the early 1800s, but died before it was complete. After remaining empty for some time it was eventually finished and occupied by John Giradot, a man who had acquired great wealth from his time with the East India Company. He was known locally as 'the Nabob', and when he went out in his magnificent coach and four, he was accompanied by a black footman, coachman and two 'spotted dogs'. In the 1820s, the estate was purchased by William Evans, whose father owned the mills at Darley Abbey. The Evans family were generous benefactors to Allestree and played an important role in community life. In 1892 the estate passed to the Gisborne family, and a few years later was leased to the Raphaels, before in 1916 coming into the possession of Colonel Johnson and his wife. They were the last of the line of lords of the manor and squires of Allestree. The picture dates to c1980.*

DCAV000724 - Picture courtesy of Derby Evening Telegraph

DRBY007874 - Picture courtesy of Derby City Council

Meynell hounds at Allestree Hall. *Allestree is situated just inside the City boundary and its park covers over 320 acres of wildlife and woodland. This c1902 picture has been taken of the Meynell Hunt in Allestree Park. It is one of the oldest and by far the largest foxhunts in the Midlands and was set up by Hugo Meynell, who also established the Quorndon Hunt in the 1770s. Hunting with hounds is no longer legal in this country. The Hall, a Grade II* listed building, partly surrounded by tall trees, provides a wonderful habitat for wildlife.*

Allestree Park. *In 1928, a firm called Commercial Construction Ltd bought Allestree Park. Although some houses were built in what are now Evans Avenue, Main Avenue and Short Avenue, they sold out to Derwent Builders, who intended to build more, but the war intervened. First the army and then the fire brigade used Allestree Hall during wartime, the latter only leaving in 1950. The Council then stepped in and bought the 323 acres of parkland including the hall. It is the wildest and most scenic of Derby's parks. The lake constructed in 1825 for Sir William Evans of Allestree Hall, partly surrounded by tall trees, provides a natural habitat for wildlife. A nine hole golf course was built in 1948 and extended to 18 holes in 1955. The park is seen here in the 1960s.*

DRBY005682 - Picture courtesy of Derby City Council

St Edmund's Church, St Edmund's Close. *The picture was taken by D Farnsworth of an 1865 engraving from Mundy Lysons' History of Derbyshire. It was not until the 1860s that St Edmund's became a parish church; previously it had been a chapel of the mother church at Mackworth. The rights of baptism, marriage and burial rested solely with the mother church. Despite only holding the status of a chapel, it had a fine 12th century doorway. The precise age of the church is uncertain, but its dedication to an Anglo-Saxon saint suggests a pre-Norman existence. When the church was rebuilt in the mid-1860s, by Stevens and Robinson of Derby, a south aisle was added and the doorway rebuilt.*

St Edmund's Church - South Porch. *Pictured is an 1865 view of the fine Norman southern entrance to the church. Another remnant of the middle ages is the yew tree, which stands in the church grounds. There is no way of knowing its precise age, although some claim it is 1,000 years old. The yew tree has strong superstitious values and the foliage has been used for burials and as a decoration at festivals in the church – Palm Sunday and Christmas. The tradition that the famous English long bow was made from yew is correct. The branches were used for practice bows, but it was heartwood from the bole which made the best bows.*

Village Pump opposite St Edmund's Close. *In ancient times a good water supply was an essential factor when selecting a site for a settlement. There was a constant supply of water off the Bunter Sandstone ridge above the village and there were several streams and springs that fed the medieval village. Long before water was piped into Allestree, there were at least four wells in the village. St Mary's Well was opposite the Red Cow, a second was at the bottom of Siddals Lane, a third opposite the old timber framed house in Cornhill and the last one which still stands today facing down St Edmund's Close.*

Red Cow, St Edmund's Close. *It is highly probable that the village inn, the Red Cow, was in existence in the early 17th century. It is shown on the 1737 map. The present building is somewhat later, the older part being late 17th century. Traditionally the pub played a major role in village life and was particularly busy when the village wakes were held. The week began with the patronal festival; this was held on the first Sunday prior to the 20th November, when the death of St Edmund, the patron saint of the church was commemorated. The wakes continued to be held until the First World War. According to legend, Lord John Manners and Dorothy Vernon stopped at a pub in Allestree, possibly the Red Cow, during their elopement, and handed over a sum of gold in exchange for food and drink from the tavern.*

DRBY000022 - Picture courtesy of Derby Evening Telegraph

St Edmund's Close. *Towards the end of the 17th Century there was much rebuilding in Allestree. The foundations of cottages in St Edmund's Close, at the top of Park Lane, and in Siddalls Lane still have the stones on which the baseplates of timber framed houses once stood. Local materials were used in the re-building adding to the charm of the old houses. Allestree's brickyard was across the Kedleston Road opposite to Allestree Lane end. Few properties survive in Allestree that are older than the 17th Century. Further along the road, just off the picture is where the village stocks used to stand by the Red Cow public house.*

DRBY003508 - Picture courtesy of Derby Evening Telegraph

Thatched cottage on Cornhill. *The name of the road was derived from the corn mill, which once stood in the vicinity. Allestree enjoyed the benefit of good, rich soil and wheat, oats and barley were grown in abundance and there were weekly corn sales. Cornhill is now part of the attractive Allestree Conservation area. This 1980 picture is of Laburnum Cottage, where in the wall of the cottage can be seen the remains of a fire place revealed when the original 17th century cottage was demolished. Close by, facing down St Edmund's Close, is the village pump and the centre of the old village.*

Palm Court Restaurant, Off Duffield Road. *The Palm Court, pictured c1980 used to be one of Derby's best restaurants, but it has been sold in the last few years for redevelopment. It was Sydney Barnes, one of the finest cricketers this country has produced, who set up the Court Café, later to become the Palm Court. He played for Staffordshire most of his career, which had only minor counties status in cricket terms, but his skill with the ball was legendary. When asked by a reporter who was the greatest bowler of all time, he replied after some hesitation, 'I think probably I was'. Many cricket experts in those days would not disagree.*

DRBY001627 - Picture courtesy of Derby Evening Telegraph

DMAG200033 - Picture courtesy of Derby Museums and Art Gallery

Duffield Road Chapel. *The first Wesleyan Chapel was situated in Church Walk, previously known as Lovers Walk. It opened in 1821 and closed in 1895, when the current Duffield Road Chapel took over; it has now been replaced by two cottages. The new chapel seen here in 1980 was largely financed by Joseph Woolley, who for some years was both Church Warden and Chapel Steward. He was a generous benefactor for missionary work abroad and made a practice of giving a shilling for each dobbie cart he made and sixpence for a wheelbarrow at his woodyard which was opposite. The cast iron milepost which stands to the right of the chapel was cast at Handysides Iron Foundry in Derby (Derby 2miles/Duffield 2miles).*

Ford Bridge over the Derwent. *The wooden bridge was built about 1886. This picture shows a steam wagon crossing the bridge, before it was rebuilt. The Portway, an ancient roadway, used to come up from near the bottom of Ford Lane on its way from Little Eaton. At first it crossed the river by a ford then by the old wooden bridge. It was referred to as Ford of Thorn Ley and for many years the track could be traced across the fields to the bottom of Park Lane, old thorn trees marking the route. It continued up Park Lane, as it is now named, and Cornhill to eventually reach Kedleston Road.*

DRBY004676 - Picture courtesy of Derby City Council

MARKEATON AND MACKWORTH

When Markeaton is mentioned, most people immediately think of Markeaton Park, with its numerous attractions and special events. It is probably the most popular park in the East Midlands with an estimated one million visitors per year and was recently placed in the 'top ten' in Europe. However, the history of Markeaton goes back much further than the date when the public park was created.

Markeaton Estate was very extensive and dominated the north–west side of Derby until the early part of the 20th century. In the Domesday Book, it was shown to be a large village with its own church and mill. The manor at that time was recorded to be in the hands of the Earl of Chester whose Steward, an ancestor of the Touchet family, controlled it.

In 1516, the manor of Markeaton, together with Mackworth and Allestree came into the hands of John Mundy, a goldsmith, who six years later became the Lord Mayor of London and was knighted in 1529. On the death of Francis Noel Mundy's widow in 1929, the estate passed to the Rev William Clark-Maxwell. The hall, built in 1755, and 16 acres of gardens were left to the Council, with the stipulation that they should be used to benefit the citizens of Derby. In addition, the council also purchased other land from Clark-Maxwell. Prior to her death, Mrs Mundy had given land to the people of Derby, where the Corporation constructed a children's play area and paddling pool, calling it 'The Mundy Playing Field'.

In the 21st century, the park is an extremely popular venue for the young and not so young. The facilities have been enhanced over the years to include a children's boating lake, amusement park, crazy golf and a miniature train ride, along with the ever popular paddling pool. During peak periods, there is a bouncy castle available, canoes, rowing boats, electric cars and donkey rides.

Mackworth Estate was developed from 1948 to 1966 and is one of the largest housing estates to be built in the city. At the time it contained a high proportion of Council Houses. Today, the majority of homes on the estate are now owner occupied, although there is still a significant stock of social housing. The housing density is quite low, with numerous areas of green open space. The main thoroughfare is Prince Charles Avenue, which is the only road on the estate not named after places in London.

A little further along the A52, on the opposite side of the road towards Asbourne, is the village of Mackworth. It has a Grade II* listed building, in the form of an unfinished late 15th century stone gatehouse, which opens into a farmyard. All Saint's Church, which stands back in the fields, dates to at least the twelfth century and is thought to be Norman in origin. Historically, the parish also contained the neighbouring village of Markeaton, which is now within Derby city boundary.

Trail: Markeaton Lane – Markeaton Hall – Markeaton Brook – Markeaton Park – Markeaton Lake – Bowbridge Fields – Mackworth Estate – Mackworth Village.

Markeaton Lane. *In September 1975, what remained of Markeaton village was designated a Conservation Area, to protect the last remnants of what was once a prosperous farming village. The small group of buildings on the western side of Markeaton Park, pictured here c1960, date from the late 18th century. Home Farm, The Green and the Farm are all of architectural and historical interest. Home Farm, opposite The Green, is a fine example of a traditional small agricultural holding, the buildings dating back to c1760. It was built by the Mundy family, to provide food and other supplies for the estate. Members of the public may visit the farm on selected dates, where a wide range of animals are kept, including some rare breeds. Seasonal attractions include hatching chicks in the incubator and newborn animals. One of the barns has been converted into a Tea Room and Gift Shop.*

DRBY007885 - Picture courtesy of Derby City Council

DRBY006036 - Picture courtesy of Derby City Council

'Markeaton Hall Derbyshire - The seat of William Mundy Esq. MP'. *The hall seen here in the mid 1800s was a brick mansion, built c 1755. Markeaton Park was originally part of the Markeaton Hall Estate, owned by the Mundy family from 1516. The estates acquired by the Mundys stretched almost into central Derby and on the death of Francis Noel Mundy's widow in 1929, the hall and sixteen acres of the gardens were left to Derby Borough Council, with the condition that they should be used to benefit the citizens of Derby. The remainder of the estate was inherited by the Reverend Prebendary William Gillchrist Clark-Maxwell, who later sold 211 acres of the park and some other land to the Council for £18,000.*

Markeaton Hall - wrought iron stairway and ornate fountain. *The original of this 1956 photograph can be found in Mundy-Lysons' History of Derbyshire, Vol. 5. The hall was in a somewhat dilapidated state when it was left to the city, after being used by the Army during the Second World War, it was eventually declared unsafe. As the Council considered the cost of restoration too high, it was demolished in mid 1964. The area where the hall once stood has been laid out as a landscaped terrace, known as Markeaton Terrace. When Army Barracks were stationed on the park during the Second World War, the building where the Markeaton train is now housed was used as the NAAFI. At that time, the car park to the front of the engine shed served as the Army Parade Ground.*

DRBY007827 - Picture courtesy of Mr M Brice

DRBY004691 - Picture courtesy of Derby Evening Telegraph

The Orangery, Markeaton Park. *The Orangery, situated near to the centre of the park, survived, when the remainder of the hall was demolished in 1964. It was designed by Joseph Pickford, the Derby architect, as part of a twin courtyard and hunting stable for F.N.C. Mundy and built around 1772. It now holds Grade II listed status and has been converted into attractive tea rooms, where weather permitting, visitors can sit outside and admire the superb flower beds. An earlier Tudor building stood on the site before it was replaced by the hall.*

Craft village, Markeaton Park. *When Markeaton Hall was demolished in 1964, the stables were retained. In 1987, they became the home of the Markeaton Craft Village, seen here two years later. It is made up of a number of individual units, where, at times, visitors are able to watch skilled craftspeople at work, making furniture, ceramics, stained glass and other products. Some of the other outbuildings have been converted for football changing rooms and there are also public toilets. They face onto the attractively renovated Domesday Mill Pond, which was the site of an early water mill.*

DRBY004690 - Picture courtesy of Derby Evening Telegraph

DRBY005827 - Picture courtesy of Hurst and Wallis

Millrace sluices on Markeaton Brook during construction of Markeaton Lake. *There was a mill at Markeaton, which pre-dates the Normans and is recorded in the Domesday Book of 1086. It was probably demolished around 1800, the last known record of the mill dating back to the map of 1760. It was not shown on the first 1" OS map, published in 1836. The mill stood immediately to the left in the trees and was fed by an embanked leat from Markeaton Brook. The wheel pit remains, but has been restored, with the wheel bearer stone still in place. The picture dates back to c1930.*

Markeaton Brook. *Markeaton Brook is noted for its clean water and the surprising wealth and variety of wildlife which it attracts, being more characteristic of a country than a city stream. It starts its journey in the Kedleston Hall Estate, three miles north-west of Derby passing through Markeaton Park, before entering the River Derwent at Bass Recreation Ground. On 24 October 2007, it was featured on BBC's Nature of Britain series, fronted by Alan Titchmarsh, looking at urban wildlife. Also featured were the Peregrine Falcons at the Cathedral, and The Sanctuary Bird and Nature Reserve at Pride Park.*

DMAG400054 - Picture courtesy of Derby Museums and Art Gallery

DRBY002757 - Picture courtesy of Derby Evening Telegraph

Waterwheel, Mill Pond. *Markeaton was fairly well endowed at the time of the Domesday Book; it had its own mill and fishponds to provide a plentiful supply of food. The wheel pit remains from the days when the mill was still in existence, with the wheel bearer stone still in place, as pictured in 1986. It now forms part of an attractive ornamental rockery with a waterfall. The former mill pond is a popular site for visitors and children in particular who enjoy watching the ducks on the pond.*

Derby Auxiliary Fire Brigade, first exercises in Markeaton Park - 13 Feb 1939. *The Auxiliary Fire Service was formed from volunteers at the outbreak of the Second World War, to assist the regular fire brigades. Fire was a huge threat to the British people. Emergency firewater tanks were installed in many towns and where a large water supply such as a river or lake was available; pipes were laid to provide water for fire fighting. The AFB were required to assist on the nights of 8/9 May 1940, after the Luftwaffe launched a major attack on Sheffield, Hull, Nottingham and Derby. Fire crews not only had to defend their own towns and cities but were expected to travel to other areas when there was a severe bombing raid.*

DRBY007812 - Picture courtesy of Derby Evening Telegraph

DRBY005830 - Picture courtesy of Hurst and Wallis

Construction of Markeaton Lake. *Markeaton Park, pictured c1930, was officially opened by the Duke of Kent in June 1931, on the same day as Darley Abbey Park. Two years later, work began to increase the size of William Emes', long thin lake, which was opened in July 1934 in a ceremony attended by thousands. At the end of the ceremony, the Mayor and other officials took a trip round the lake in a motor boat. The old water mill was powered by water from Markeaton Brook, which now forms the source of the man-made lake. It was dug out by crane and manual labour as a means of providing work during the depression of the 1930s.*

Bowbridge Fields - Emes' House. *Bowbridge Fields, pictured in 1990, was the family home of William Emes, which he rebuilt about 1760. He was employed as a gardener at Kedleston Hall in 1756. Four years later, when Robert Adam was given responsibility for management of the entire grounds, he left his post to work for himself. Whilst at Kedleston he had started to alter the earlier formal nature of the park and had constructed the upper lake. During his career as a landscape gardener, the main features of his designs were trees and water. He also designed a few minor buildings.*

DMAG200242 - Picture courtesy of Derby Museums and Art Gallery

DRBY004462 - Picture courtesy of Derby City Council

Westbourne Park, Mackworth Estate. *This April 1952 view of the construction work in progress on the Mackworth Estate shows the Westbourne Park section under development. Mackworth lies off the busy A52 Derby to Ashbourne road, on the opposite side of the highway to Markeaton Park. Most of this large suburb, of mainly council houses, was built in the 1950s, but in recent years many of the properties have passed into private ownership. It has little connection with the village which bears the same name a short distance away on the opposite side of the A52. One of Derby's celebrities, Julia Watson, who played Baz in Casualty for many years, although originating from South Wales, spent some of her school days in Mackworth. Her family lived at Westbourne Park.*

Mackworth Minstrels at Parkfields School. *A happy picture taken in 1983 of Mackworth Minstrels proudly lined up behind a table laden with trophies. Mackworth was developed during the 1950s; the first house being completed in 1953. The estate used to be home to Derby College, on Prince Charles Avenue Campus. The college then comprised of buildings which were formerly Mackworth Secondary School and Parkfields Cedars Girls Grammar School. They subsequently combined to form Parkfields Comprehensive School, but this closed in the 1980s.*

DRBY002510 - Picture courtesy of Derby Evening Telegraph

DRBY007887 - Picture courtesy of Derby Local Studies Library

Mackworth Gatehouse. *The Gatehouse, seen here c1881, is a Grade a Grade II* listed building, located in a sunken road running through the old village of Mackworth. It was intended to form the entrance to the De Mackworth family seat and is frequently referred to as Mackworth Castle, but no castle was ever built. The family having inherited an estate in Rutland went to live there instead and the house was never completed. The gatehouse now opens into a farmyard. Originally, a timber-framed fortified Manor House probably stood on the site, which, it is said, was destroyed during the English Civil War.*

All Saints Church, Mackworth. *The church mentioned in the Domesday Book was possibly the one at Markeaton, but it is almost certain there was a church at Mackworth in 1200. It was restored in 1851, but parts of the building are 13th and 14th century. The church stands back from the road, isolated in a field to the east of the village centre. It was built alongside Long Lane, the Derby to Rocester Roman Road. According to Pevsner, the west tower is 'supposed to have defensive purposes'. Also the nave can be barred and there are only small windows on the lower levels. Cross bow loop holes on the north and west of the tower add substance to Pevsner's argument. The picture dates from 1855.*

DRBY007888 - Picture courtesy of Derby Local Studies Library

CHAPTER 9 - CHADDESDEN, OAKWOOD AND SPONDON

CHADDESDEN AND OAKWOOD

Chaddesden which the locals like to call 'Chad' is one of Derby's largest suburbs. Until the early 1900s, it was a small independent village in the countryside like several others that surrounded Derby. However, boundary changes in 1901, 1928, 1934 and finally in 1968, resulted in many villages being absorbed into the county town completely losing their identities as a result. Present day Chaddesden is a mixture of modern housing and older council houses, many of which are now privately owned. The estates mostly comprise of properties built in the early 1950s as poor quality housing in Derby's West End was cleared.

The first written evidence of Chaddesden's existence is in the Domesday Book, when 26 families were recorded living there, with a total population of around 100. At that time the village formed part of Spondon, and it was not until after a chapel was built in Chaddesden in the 14th century that the diocesan bishop gave the right to bury the dead in the churchyard and not at the church in Spondon. Prior to that, the dead had to be carried to Spondon across Chaddesden Brook, which was prone to flooding, thus rendering the journey impossible at times. Permission was only granted on the condition that the fees should still go to the vicar of the mother church.

In 1839, the Midland Counties Railway installed the line from Nottingham through the area, but it was not until the early 1900s that major changes started to occur. In 1901 the fifth baronet, Sir Henry Wilmot, died and the house was inherited by his nephew: the baronet's sister continued to live there until she died in 1916. A few years later the estate was sold and the house demolished. This provided the council with the opportunity they were looking for to purchase land for re-housing purposes. Some land was also purchased by private developers.

In 1921, Chaddesden's population was 560 but, by 1961, it had risen to 15,622. Its close proximity to Derby and improving communication facilities were crucial factors which made the location a very attractive one. The railway industry and its numerous suppliers were mostly on the eastern side of the town, which meant for many Chaddesden residents that it was relatively easy to get to work. The former site of Chaddesden Hall and some of the parkland, now known as Chaddesden Park, was retained and leased to the Parish Council, later to be purchased by the Borough Council.

One of the few open spaces remaining on the north east side of Chaddesden was acquired in the 1980s for development. Despite local opposition, permission was granted for a new estate to be built and named Oakwood. Fortunately, Chaddesden Wood survived and still retains its old name despite now being part of Oakwood. It covers 23 acres and is home to the only ancient oak woodland in Derby. In April 1991, it was declared a Local Nature Reserve. As a result of the action taken, wildlife will be protected and it will be of considerable value to future generations for recreational and educational purposes.

Trail: Chaddesden Park – Morley Road – Chaddesden Lane – Chaddesden Sidings – Racecourse Ground.

Chaddesden Hall. *Chaddesden Hall is where the Wilmot family lived for nearly three centuries. It dominated the village and was the last in a series of houses built by the family. Edward Wilmot inherited the estate in 1727, and set about building a replacement house made from brick and stone. He was made a baronet in 1759. Further extensions and improvements were added by subsequent generations and the gardens landscaped. In 1901, Sir Henry Wilmot died. As he did not have any children, the house was inherited by a nephew and after the baronet's sister died in 1916, the estate was divided up and sold. The house was demolished and the Council acquired part of the land for development, preserving the remainder for public recreation.*

DRBY003858 - Picture courtesy of Derby City Council

DRBY003835 - Picture courtesy of Derby City Council

***Chaddesden Park**. Following the death of Sir Henry Wilmot's sister in 1916, the estate was divided up in the early 1920s and sold. The site of the hall and some of the parkland was retained and leased to the Parish Council to be used as a public amenity. A park was created, running in a north to south direction from Maine Drive to Nottingham Road, which caters for a variety of activities. These include an outdoor children's paddling pool, crown green bowling, football and cricket pitches. The woodland in the park is a mix of mature trees with a stream running through the centre. This c1935 picture shows adults and children enjoying a stroll by the brook, which runs through the park.*

***Chaddesden Park Carnival, 1990**. A very popular event held on an annual basis is Chaddesden Carnival, referred to locally as 'The Big One'. In the picture the Derbyairs Carnival Band are seen marching at the carnival in 1990. A comprehensive list of events takes place every year in the park, which is situated off Nottingham Road, with vehicle access by Chaddesden Lane to Maine Drive, where there is a car park. There are large open grassed areas suitable for a variety of recreational activities and a picnic area.*

DRBY005117 - Picture courtesy of Derby Evening Telegraph

DRBY003301 - Picture courtesy of Derby City Council

St Mary's Church, Chaddesden. *This pre 1865 view of the East end of St Mary's Church was taken from Mundy Lyson's, vol. 6. Until 1347, St Mary's Church was one of the chapelries attached to the mother church at Spondon. At that time villagers applied to the Bishop for the right to bury their own dead. They pointed out that Chaddesden Brook frequently flooded, which often prevented corpses being taken to Spondon for burial. The Bishop agreed to the request, but on condition that the fees should still go to the vicar of the mother church. Pevsner says it was rebuilt as a college or chantry foundation c1357 by Henry Chaddesden, Archdeacon of Leicester.*

DRBY007594 - Picture courtesy of Derby City Council

St Mary's Church - Rood Screen, Chancel and East Window. *This c1902 view of the east end of St Mary's Church was taken from Mundy Lyson's, vol. 6. It is a Grade A listed church one of only two in Derby, situated in an attractive location looking down on Chaddesden Park. The chancel is particularly impressive and is reached through a 15th century rood screen. The large east window was installed in 1857-58. However, huge sections of this were destroyed in 1940, by bombs falling on Chaddesden Park, during the Second World War.*

DRBY003825 - Picture courtesy of Derby City Council

Ivy Cottage, Jasmine Cottage and Beech Cottage, Chaddesden Lane. *For many years Chaddesden, or 'Chad' as the locals like to call it, remained a small village. The Wilmots were squires of the village for nearly three centuries and held large tracts of the land, which for a time prevented building incursions into the area. This all changed with the sale of the hall and land in the 1920s. Although some of the older houses still remain, mainly along Chaddeden Lane and Morley Road. Ivy Cottage, Jasmine and Beech cottages still line Chaddesden Lane as seen in 1890. The outbuildings of Jasmine Cottage were once used as an animal slaughterhouse for Mr F Oldershaw's Butcher's shop. Ivy and Beech cottages had covered areas providing shelter for horses.*

Chaddesden Lane. *Shortly after Chaddesdn Hall had been demolished in the late 1920s, new houses were built along the lane. This c1935 picture shows the recently built houses along the western edge of Chaddesden Lane. The lane eventually becomes Morley Road, where situated on the corner of Chapel Lane, is the Wilmot Arms pubic house. It has been in existence at least since 1770 and was originally called the Wheel, but as it was near the church and hall, it was later re-named the Wilmot Arms. At one time it was the main pub in the old village. Further along Morley Road is the vast new estate of Oakwood, built in the late 1900s for the most part in the former Parish of Chaddeden. It is composed mainly of privately owned houses, which differs somewhat from Chaddesden where a large proportion of the housing stock started life as council houses, although many have subsequently been purchased.*

DRBY000170 - Picture courtesy of Derby City Council

DRBY000171 - Picture courtesy of Derby City Council

Alms Houses Chaddesden. *The inhabitants from the Wilmot Almshouses, opposite the church, have come out to find out what is going on when this picture was taken c1900. The six, tiny, timber framed almshouses were built around 1638, as part of the Wilmot Charity bequest. They provided homes for four poor men and two poor women. A requirement of occupancy was that the inhabitants had to wear the livery of their benefactor, which was black trimmed with silver. This led to the almshouses often being referred to as the 'Black Hospital.' They were condemned as unfit for human habitation in 1956 and demolished seven years later.*

Chaddesden Sidings. *The former railway wagon repair shop pictured in 1987 has in recent years become the premises of the Derby Fireplace Company. Originally it formed part of Chaddesden Sidings, which were sited alongside the former Midland Counties route into Derby. Here were constructed reception sidings, sorting, cripple and repair sidings, a workshop, turntables and so on. However, the opening on 27 June 1867 of a more suitable route resulted in most passenger traffic being diverted to avoid the need for the trains to reverse. As a result the sidings became redundant.*

DRBY005140 - Picture courtesy of Derby Evening Telegraph

DRBY007577 - Picture courtesy of Derby Evening Telegraph

Wyvern Centre development site - opening ceremony, April 1991. *Most of the old Chaddesden Sidings site has been redeveloped as the Wyvern Business Centre. It was given its name, because the Wyvern, a mythical griffon like beast, was the symbol of the Midland Railway. Prior to the arrival of the railways in 1839, the area on the northern side of the River Derwent was called The Meadows and, as the name suggests, was originally farmland. But with the arrival of the railway in 1839, a major part of the land was taken over by the railway industry and became known as Chaddesden Sidings. In recent years, sand and gravel has been extracted from a site on the western side of the Wyvern for the building industry.*

Derby Race Course, Nottingham Road. *After losing out to the rapidly expanding railways, racing was re-established on land to the east of Derby Canal. The first meeting took place in May 1848. The stand was designed by Henry Duesbury and replaced in 1911 by a larger one. The last meeting was held on 9 August 1939, when Gordon Richards (later Sir Gordon} rode one of the winners. The Racecourse Ground has been the home, and still is, of Derbyshire County Cricket Club, which was established in 1870. The picture dates back to c1860.*

DRBY003224 - Picture courtesy of Derby City Council

DRBY000257 - Picture courtesy of Derby Evening Telegraph

Michael Holding signs for Derbyshire County Cricket Club. *Roger Pearman, the Derbyshire County Cricket Club Chief Executive, watches Michael Holding, widely acknowledged as one of the fastest and best bowlers in cricket history, sign a contract to play for the county. In 60 tests for the West Indies he took 249 wickets at an average 23.68. Holding played for Derbyshire from 1983 to 1989 taking 224 first class wickets for the county at an average of 24.57. He held the Derbyshire record for the best bowling performance in a one day match, taking 8-21 in a Nat-West trophy match against Sussex in 1988, enabling the county to get to the Benson Hedges final.*

Chaddesden Home Guards. *The above picture was taken in 1942 outside the old Council House in Derby of officers and non-commissioned officers. Although many men became national servicemen during the Second World War, it was essential that others stayed at home to help run the country. In this respect some men were deemed to have reserved occupations, which were considered so important they could not join the forces. These included engineering, farming, medicine and civilian administration all of which the authorities decided came into this category. Many of these men joined the Home Guard, which was formed to prepare for possible invasion by enemy troops.*

DRBY003838 - Picture courtesy of Derby City Council

SPONDON

Spondon was once a quiet farming village, dating back to at least Anglo-Saxon days. Now it is a prosperous suburb of Derby, bisected by the busy A52 Derby to Nottingham bypass, four miles to the east of the city centre.

The greatest upheaval in the village's history came in 1340, when Spondon was nearly wiped out because of a disastrous fire caused by a woman drying malt at the door of a furnace. The fire raged out of control and spread quickly in a high wind. The church was destroyed and almost all the houses suffered the same fate, other than one or two on the windward side of the fire. The devastation was so great that the villagers appealed to the King for support and he granted them relief from the payment of taxes.

The Malt Shovel Inn now stands on the site where the malting house once stood, where the fire originated. This has led to the claim that it is the oldest site of any public house within Derby. The present inn has been rebuilt twice, parts of which date back to 1680.

Following the fire, the village gradually recovered and although it remained for many years a predominantly farming community, other industries sprang up including basket making, a timber yard (in what was then appropriately called Saw Pit Lane, now West Road), a brick yard, a boot repairers and a blacksmith. The women were kept busy winding cotton onto bobbins. The cotton was delivered weekly to the White Swan Inn from the mills at Darley Abbey.

Prior to the Industrial Revolution, Spondon became famous for making silk gloves. The silk being collected from Nottingham and a week later returned in the form of gloves. All the family were involved in this cottage industry and there were a large number of spinning-frames in the village at that time, some used to make silk stockings.

In 1779, the canal brought prosperity to Spondon, and the arrival of the railway 60 years later soon made Spondon a popular place to live and a number of large houses were constructed. Senior Railway Officials occupied several of the properties.

There has been an industrial site on the banks of the River Derwent at Spondon since 1916, originally established during the First World War, to waterproof aircraft wings. The site-commenced production under the name of British Cellulose and Chemical Manufacturing Company and since then has operated under various names including British Celanese and Courtaulds. In 2007, it was acquired by Celanese again, but sadly on the 28 April 2010, the Derby Telegraph announced 'Celanese driven out by soaring price of energy'.

Trail: Sitwell Street – Potter Street – Royal Hill Road – Locko Road – Chapel Street – Church Street – Lodge Lane – Megaloughton Lane.

Blacksmiths, Sitwell Street. *For many years Spondon was a farming community, but during the 19th century other new businesses sprang up. This increased the need for horse power, on the farm and within the village to move heavy loads as well as for transporting people. As a result the local village blacksmith was much in demand. The smithy was in Sitwell Street, where two horses are being shoed in the c1900s picture. The Coxon family were for many generations the village blacksmiths. Peter Coxon Junior was additionally listed as the landlord of the White Swan. Outside the smithy was the village pump, where residents went to collect water.*

DRBY007480 - Picture courtesy of Derby City Council

DRBY002340 - Picture courtesy of Derby Evening Telegraph

The Homestead, Sitwell Street. *The Homestead is a magnificent Grade I listed building, dated 1740, and considered to be one of the finest Georgian buildings in Derbyshire. It has been well maintained and retains many of its original features the stone gate piers are particularly impressive. It was built for Jonathan Anthill, the owner of a local tannery and lived in by his brother who left it to his niece. She married the vicar of Spondon, Rev. John Cade, and their son became a well known Derby surgeon. His wife was the daughter of Joseph Wright the celebrated Derby artist. The Cade family stayed there for over 100 years and after that it has passed through a number of hands, including Sir Henry Fowler, Chief Engineer for the London Midland and Scottish Railway. It was sold by Courtauld's in 1996 after 77 years and converted into a restaurant, but this closed in 2003. The picture was taken in 1980.*

DRBY007409 - Picture courtesy of Derby Evening Telegraph

The Malt Shovel public house, Potter Street. *The greatest upheaval in the village's history came in 1340, when Spondon was nearly wiped out because of a disastrous fire caused by a woman drying malt at the door of a furnace. The fire raged out of control and spread quickly in a high wind. The church was destroyed and almost all the houses suffered the same fate, other than one or two on the windward side of the fire. The Malt Shovel Inn, pictured in 1987, now stands on the site where the malting house once stood from where the fire originated. The present inn has been rebuilt twice, parts of which date back to 1680.*

Spondon Cricket Club, Royal Hill Road, Off Locko Road. *An early 20th century picture of a Spondon Cricket Club team at their Royal Hill Road Ground. The club was founded in 1883 and remained on the same site until the early years of the 21st century. Following the purchase of the ground for housing development, the club moved to a new headquarters further north up Locko Road. The club currently has five senior teams and a number of junior sides. In recent times Spondon Cricket Club has achieved notable success in the Derbyshire Premier League including winning the division one title in 2007. Close by the old ground stands Mill Row, formerly a row of stockingers cottages. The village windmill also stood nearby.*

DRBY001588 - Picture courtesy of Derby City Council

DRBY007891 - Picture courtesy of Derby City Council

South front of Locko Park from the south west. *Built in the 1720s by Francis Smith of Warwick, Locko Hall, pictured in May 1898 has been the ancestral home of the Drury-Lowe family since 1747. A chapel was first built on the site in 1669, prior to that in medieval times a leper hospital occupied the land. William Emes was responsible for the park design, though the actual work was undertaken by his partner John Webb. In August each year it used to host the Novice and Intermediate Horse Trial Championships of Great Britain, in which Princess Anne and many other well known riders have participated.*

Locko Hall - Picture Gallery. *In the 1850s Henry Stevens, a local architect was commissioned to embellish Locko in Italian style, many of the additions and alterations being made for the sole purpose of housing and showing off the paintings. As a result the house has strong Italianate features, which reflects the taste of William Drury-Lowe who made many visits to Italy in the mid 1800s, bringing back some 300 important works of art. His eldest son, William Nathaniel Drury-Lowe continued the refurbishment of the Locko Hall. He commissioned an Italianate painted ceiling to complement both the house and paintings. The picture gallery is seen here in 1912.*

DRBY002355 - Picture courtesy of Derby City Council

DCHQ500201 - Picture courtesy of A P Knighton

Chapel Street. *There have been Methodist Chapels in Spondon since the beginning of the 19th century. The present chapel, opened in 1934, and is to be found on the corner of Lodge Lane. The Jehovah's Witness Hall, in Chapel Street, now occupies the site of the old Methodist Chapel of 1877. In the same street, the former Village School is at present the home of the Derby School of Bridge. The picture shows the Prince of Wales pub and, also the White Swan at the junction with Sitwell Street. During the mid 1800s, church services were held at the White Swan every fifth Sunday, when the vicar was away taking services at Stanley and Locko. Hence, the name 'missed Sunday' was commonly used, when there was no service in church. This picture was taken in the early 1900s.*

Church Street, decorated for the wedding of Sir Richard Cooper and Alice Priestland. *This picture has been taken from the top of the church tower, in 1900, of a busy scene in Church Street. It is one of a collection, inherited by the family of the Rev Edward Andreas Priestland, one time Master of the Gentleman's School, Church Street, and later curate at Spondon Church. The occasion being celebrated by the people in the street is the marriage of his eldest daughter to Sir Richard Cooper. Sir Richard was one of the Reverend's pupils, who it is said, vowed to return to marry Alice.*

DRBY007743 - Picture courtesy of A P Knighton

DRBY001496 - Picture courtesy of Don Farnsworth

Saxon cross, St Werburgh's Church. *The Anglo-Saxon cross, which stands in the grounds of the church, is designated as a Scheduled Ancient Monument. It is the only one found in the county made of limestone, which tends to chip easily because of the fossil content. The curious design on the cross is thought to be Celtic in origin. There is ample evidence of Anglo-Saxon and Danish settlements in the Derwent Valley and the cross denotes there was early Christian activity at Spondon. Probably even before the end of the seventh century during which the Mercian Kings accepted Christianity. The picture was taken in 1972.*

Church Street, Spondon. *Looking along Church Street, c1920s, towards St Werburgh's Church, one of only a small number in the country dedicated to the Saxon Saint, Werburgh. The church was for many years known as St Mary's, but was later discovered to be dedicated to St Werburgh. There was a church in Spondon at the time of the Domesday Survey, but about 100 years later it was given to the Burton Lazars Monastery by William de Ferrers, Earl of Derby. They built a hospital for lepers in the hamlet of Locko. Tragedy occurred in the great fire 1340, when the church and most of the village was burnt down. The church was rebuilt and restored in 1826 and also 1892. A low window in the south wall is said to have been used as squint by the lepers from Locko.*

DRBY007477 - Picture courtesy of Derby City Council

DRBY007893 - Picture courtesy of Derby City Council

Lodge Cottage, Lodge Lane. *This attractive thatched cottage, pictured c1920 was built around 1785 on the corner of the Derby to Nottingham road. It acted for a number of years as a forwarding station for mail, which was collected by coaches travelling between Derby and Nottingham. An increase in traffic caused by the British Celanese company had led to considerable congestion and the need to widen the road. As a result the lodge was demolished in 1929. but its memory lives on through the name of the road, Lodge Lane.*

British Cellulose Company, Megaloughton Lane. *The site was built in 1914 during the First World War when two Swiss chemists, the Dreyfus brothers, set up the British Cellulose and Chemical Manufacturing Company to make a lacquer to waterproof aircraft wings. They were the first commercial producers of cellulose acetate flake. It was later realised that a special production method would produce a textile yarn with unique qualities which made it look like silk, but cost a fraction of the price. In 1925, the company became the hugely-successful British Celanese, which by the 1940s had a workforce of 18,000 as its product range expanded to include fabric for parachutes. British Celanese was purchased by Courtaulds in 1961. They were pioneers of manmade fibre production and one of the first companies to make cellulose acetate. Production of textile yarns and flake started in Coventry in 1927. Courtaulds in turn was bought by Dutch group Akzo Nobel in 1998. A year later a buy-out by venture capitalists with the management set up Acordis. In 2007, Celanese acquired the company again, and the name changed to Celanese Acetate Limited. Sadly on the 28 April 2010 the Derby Telegraph headline, announced 'Celanese driven out by soaring price of energy.'*

DRBY001405 - Picture courtesy of Derby City Council

CHAPTER 10 - CHELLASTON TO OSMASTON

CHELLASTON AND SHELTON LOCK

Chellaston was once mainly a farming community, but is now a rapidly expanding suburb, like so many more up and down the country, where houses proliferate close to busy road networks. In Chellaston's case the expansion of Derby and the recent opening of the A50, giving it rapid access to fast roads and the M1 Motorway, have led to the growth of massive housing developments.

The story of Chellaston though is not just one of a once quiet village expanding rapidly because of its location. From the Middle Ages it became internationally famous as the centre of the English alabaster industry, a form of gypsum. It was at its peak between about 1360 and 1460, when a flourishing export trade developed. Great blocks of alabaster were taken to the River Trent and then transported by boat to Hull, for shipment across the North Sea.

The alabaster produced at the Woodlands Quarry in Chellaston, now an area where wildlife thrives, was particularly attractive and easy to carve. The purest white alabaster was originally found close to the surface and that made it easily accessible to work. Coloured deposits were found deeper down and used until new layers of white alabaster were located.

Over 3,000 alabaster carvings have been identified overseas, a large collection of which have been recovered and are now in the Victoria and Albert Museum, most of which probably started life in Chellaston. In the warmer, drier countries like Spain, alabaster could be preserved out of doors, but the wetter, colder climate experienced in this country forced its use inside.

The Act of 1550, which banned mass books and images, but not tombstones, reduced the level of output in the industry. The trade died with the Reformation, but sprang up again briefly in the late Victorian era, when a pulpit was carved for Worcester Cathedral and monuments for Westminster Abbey and Eton College Chapel. Good quality alabaster was not found in large quantities after the Second World War, but gypsum was extracted until 1978, when the pit finally closed down.

Shelton Lock is a small suburb to the south of Derby City centre, located between Chellaston and Allenton. Derby Canal once ran through the area, but the only traces of the canal's existence are seen in the form of a road bridge, the lock stones, and a cycle path which covers it. Following the closure of the canal in 1964, it was filled in and the cycle track created. The site of Fullen's Lock is located a short distance down the cycle path from Shelton Lock Bridge. A children's playground close to the site still bears the name.

Trail: High Street – Brick Works (Woodlands Quarry) – Derby Road – Station Road – Shelton Lock

DRBY003196 - Picture courtesy of R E Pearson

High Street. *High Street, viewed in 1974 from the Derby Road end, looking towards the church in the distance. St Peter's Church dates back to the medieval period, but radical alterations were carried out in the 19th century. It has a Norman font, but surprisingly, it did not have any alabaster ornamentation for many years, until the author of a book on the subject gave the church a small carved replica of St Peter's. The lack of ornamentation arose in 1817, when the church was restored and a churchwarden used the alabaster slabs to pave his stable floor! Alabaster, on the other hand, at the Methodist Chapel is well represented.*

DRBY002109 - Picture courtesy of Derby City Council

High Street. *This is an earlier c1930 view of High Street taken from a postcard, looking along the street towards St Peter's Church. Burdett's map of 1767, showed only one or two buildings along High Street and this had changed only a little by the time the Ordnance Survey published its first map of the area. High Street was then the main street in the village and still remains today unchanged in length and shape, although the road has been widened and proper pavements created. In recent years the population of Chellaston has expanded rapidly, particularly since it was absorbed by Derby in 1968.*

DRBY000097 - Picture courtesy of Derby City Council

John Forman's House, High Street. *This is another view of High Street, this time c1905, which shows John Forman's wife and a grandchild with its mother, standing in the doorway of the family shop. Forman kept the village grocery shop and this picture has been taken shortly after it has been renovated. The roof had been tiled replacing the original thatch, new windows installed, the property repainted and stucco added to the ground floor wall. The Formans were prominent figures in both the village and Derby, John's cousin Robert, served as Mayor in Derby in 1848 and his son, Thomas, twenty years later. Henry Forman who lived at the Yews was also an important business man.*

DMAG000715 - Picture courtesy of Derby Museums and Art Gallery

***Horse and cart** at Chellaston **Brick** Works. During the First World War there was a considerable increase in demand for bricks, when Chellaston Brick Works was in the ownership of Woodlands Farm. After the war the works were modernised by adding a new Hoffman Kiln, and the old steam engine was replaced with a much more efficient gas engine. Trade though declined and following changes of the ownership, by 1923, John Williamson and F.W. Gilbert had taken control. Up until then bricks were delivered by horse and cart, but this changed when the decision was made to contract T.W. Napper to convey the bricks in his three lorries.*

***Brick Lorry at Chellaston Brick Works.** A lorry loaded with bricks in the mid 1920s about to set off on a delivery. In 1925, Chellaston Minerals, as the company was then called, decided it would be more efficient to have their own vehicle rather than contract out all their work. They purchased a Leyland lorry from T.W.Napper. This vehicle helped the company expand their business into other counties, including Lincolnshire, Northamptonshire and Warwickshire. The production of bricks remained very much the same, but the new machinery installed in the 1920s considerably increased capacity. The driver of the first company lorry in 1925 was Mr. G Sault, who remained with the company until retirement in 1970.*

DMAG000717 - Picture courtesy of Derby Museums and Art Gallery

DMAG000716 - Picture courtesy of Derby Museums and Art Gallery

The Staff at Chellaston Brick Works. *Several Chellaston families had long connections with the works, the Smithurst family in particular, of whom William Henry also found time to run the Red Lion public house in the village. Chellaston 'named' bricks were hand produced and have been used to build many 'council' houses in Derby, particularly in the 1930s. In the years leading up to closure in 1977, the works produced mainly 'common' bricks. They were cheaper to make and the output was much greater. The 1953 figures showed a normal weekly yield of common bricks of 120,000, compared with the approximate figure of 200 per day for Chellaston bricks. Note the two kilns in the background of this mid 1920s picture.*

Chellaston Infants School, School Lane. *A co-educational school for children aged from four to seven years, which is maintained by Derby City Council. It was opened in 1878 for the education of children of all ages. However, in January 1967 it became an Infant School following the opening of Chellaston Junior School. Crow Tree House, 32 School Lane, a double-fronted red brick dwelling adjacent to the school is the house where the Gresley family lived. Harold Gresley, who was born in 1892, lived all his life in Chellaston, and along with his brother Cuthbert, father Frank and grandfather James, he was a landscape painter. After serving in the First World War, he studied at Nottingham School of Art and during 1925-26 created a series of Derby townscapes that later became part of the Goodey Collection. In addition, he produced many views of Derbyshire beauty spots and country houses.*

DRBY000095 - Picture courtesy of Derby Evening Telegraph

DCHQ501623 - Picture courtesy of A P Knighton

New Inn, Derby Road. *This c1908 picture has been taken looking down Swarkestone Road, with Station Road on the right and High Street on the left. The New Inn can be clearly seen on the right, with the Rose and Crown, the oldest pub in the village with its thatched roof further along the road. Pym's shop is on the left. The New Inn opened in 1863, but may have replaced an earlier inn. After the Second World War its name was changed to the Corner Pin. A cruck timber-framed building, it had its cruck timbers restored in 2002.*

Former Derby to Melbourne and Ashby Railway Line. *Formerly, Chellaston had its own railway station, which was situated at the bottom of Station Road, but little trace of the site exists today. The station's full name was Chellaston and Swarkestone. The line was opened in 1867, but closed in 1982. Local people found the line particularly useful on Friday each week to visit Derby on Market Day. During the Second World War, the line was taken over by the War Department and used as a railway training centre. Following the closure, the track has been converted by Sustrans, into a footpath and cycle track. The horses in the picture belonged to gypsies encamped in the vicinity.*

DCHQ001905 - Picture courtesy of David Birt

DMAG000541 - Picture courtesy of Derby Museums and Art Gallery

Derby Canal, Shelton Lock and lock keepers cottage. *The Derby Canal Act was passed on the 7 May 1793 and the canal was constructed under the supervision of the engineer, Benjamin Outram. It was 14 miles long and ran from a junction with the Erewash Canal at Sandiacre, to a junction with the Trent and Mersey Canal at Swarkestone. It was officially opened on the 30 June 1796 and is pictured here c1935. A passenger boat was in operation at the time and it carried people from Swarkestone to Derby every Friday for market day. Improvements in road transport saw business decline and it was abandoned in 1964. Derby and Sandiacre Canal Trust and Society plan to restore the canal as a navigable waterway.*

The (New) Bridge Inn, Chellaston Road, Shelton Lock. *Shelton Lock got part of its name from a local landowner, Joseph Shelton, who built a wharf close to Chellaston Road Bridge. This became known as 'Shelton's Wharf' and on the other side of the road stood a canal lock and lock-keepers cottage. The original beerhouse located by the canal bridge was called the Shelton Lock Inn, but later became the Bridge Inn. This was eventually replaced by the present building and in due course the word 'New' was added. Bert Mozley, the famous Derby and England footballer, played for a short time for Shelton United, whose ground was behind the Bridge Inn.*

DRBY006406 - Picture courtesy of Derby Museum & Art Gallery

ALVASTON TO OSMASTON

Alvaston existed well before 1086 when the Domesday Book was published. There was a church there in Saxon times as the discovery of a Saxon coffin lid embedded in the medieval church building proved. It remained a small village until the end of the 19th century when it started to expand, but lost Crewton from the parish. Another change took place on the 25 March 1884 when Alvaston was merged with Boulton as a single parish. Crewton was absorbed by Derby Corporation in 1901 and the rest in 1928 and 1934, apart from a few outliers which were not taken over until 1968.

Allenton, originally a small village sprang up as a speculative venture, when a man named Isaac Allen purchased several acres of land on both sides of the Derby to Swarkestone Road and began to build. The area at that time went under the name of Allentown. By 1903, 150 houses had been built and the Crown Hotel. In 1880 a school was opened.

On the south side of Allenton is the War Memorial village, a cluster of over 30 homes in a pleasant setting, built after the end of the Second World War.

The 1928 Borough Extension Act enabled the County Borough of Derby to make a start on the Ring Road, which virtually divided Alvaston into two parts. This was the signal for large scale housing development to begin. Today, both Allenton and Alvaston have busy shopping centres, with the former having a lively outdoor market on Fridays and Saturdays. Alvaston Park off the A6, backs on to the River Derwent, covers 85 acres and is a popular place for recreation.

Wilmorton is a suburb of Derby, situated between Alvaston and Osmaston, along the A6 to the south of the city centre. It was formerly part of the estate of Osmaston Hall, before being released in the 1880s and built on primarily by the Midland Railway for its Carriage, Wagon and Locomotive works. It got its name in part from the previous landowner the Reverend Sir George Wilmot-Horton.

Osmaston, which was mentioned in the Domeday Book, was once a tiny village. By the 17th century the Osmaston Estate was in the hands of the Wilmot family who built Osmaston Hall. Another branch of the same family resided at Chaddesden Hall. The family moved to Catton Hall in the 1849s, after inheriting it from the Hortons. They first let the hall to the Fox family, before selling it and the land to the Midland Railway, who used the hall as an office and built on parts of the estate. The estate is now mainly built up, but a pleasant park and sports stadium on the southern side of Osmaston Park Road provides a welcome green space.

Trail: Alvaston – Litchurch – Allenton – Osmaston

DRBY007520 - Picture courtesy of Derby City Council

St Michael's and All Angels Church, Alvaston Street. *This 1858 picture was taken soon after the church had been rebuilt, by H.I.Stevens at a cost of £2,200. It is perpendicular in style, and consists of a chancel, nave, north and south aisles, and western tower containing two bells. The register commences in 1614, and the communion plate bears the date 1662. In the porch are two very ancient sepulchral slabs found under the foundations of the old tower, which fell in 1775. One slab bears an incised cross with a circular head, the other a plain cross, which is said to be Saxon in origin.*

DRBY001624 - Picture courtesy of Derby City Council

Old Cottages and St Michael's Church, Alvaston Street. *This early 1900s picture was taken looking down Alvaston Street, towards St Michael's and All Angels Church. There has been a church and priest here at least since the time of the Domesday Survey. Disaster struck the church on the 17 August 1856, when just as the morning service was drawing to a close, the gable end of the church gave way, and the casing fell into the churchyard. This caused a premature end to the service but, fortunately, no one was hurt. The church was rebuilt and rededicated two years later. Joseph Holder, the local chimney sweep lived in the ancient cottage on the right for many years.*

The Rex Cinema, Alvaston. *Boarded up and for sale in this 1982 picture, the cinema opened its doors on the 2 March 1925, when it was known as the Alvaston Picture House. The first film to be shown starred Lionel Barrymore in Decameron Nights. It was taken over in 1939 and upgraded during a two week closure, reopening on the 10 August that year as the Rex Cinema. Declining attendances led to its closure on the 22 October 1966, after showing Seven Brides for Seven Brothers. After that it was re-opened as a full time bingo hall, but film shows were held on Saturday mornings for children and on Sunday mornings Bollywood films were screened for the Asian community. Following serving as a nightclub and a 'Fun Club', it was burnt down by vandals and demolished in 1983.*

DRBY002576 - Picture courtesy of Derby City Council

DRBY001379 - Picture courtesy of Derby City Council

Alvaston Park. *Alvaston Park shown here in the early 1900s is a public open space, backing onto the River Derwent. Thirty acres of the land was given by William Curzon of Breedon Hall, in 1910. It was landscaped by William Barron and Son of Borrowash, whose founder laid out Elvaston Castle Park for Lord Harrington. It opened to the public three years later. In 1923, a five acre lake was added and after the Second World War an extra 61.8 acres of land to the south was converted into playing fields. The former Wilmorton College (Derby College) site on the western side of the park has been converted into a housing development.*

Derby Tramways Company Horse Bus Number 4, Brighton Road. *At the end of May 1879, a provisional order was sanctioned by the House of Commons, under the Tramways Act of 1870, enabling Derby to operate a tram system. The first section of tramway to be completed was along London Road to the Midland Railway Station. Pictured in the late 1800s is Derby Tramways Company Horse Bus Number 4 standing in the yard of the depot at Alvaston. This was situated at the junction of Wildsmith Street and Brighton Road and was used exclusively for the company's horse buses. Number 4 was built in 1888 and was still in service when the company was taken over by Derby Corporation in 1899.*

DMAG001545 - Picture courtesy of Derby Museums and Art Gallery

DRBY004592 - Picture courtesy of Derby City Council

Building Locomotives at Derby Locomotive Works. *The Midland Railway Company acquired a small site in 1840 and built workshops to repair their rail vehicles. This site soon expanded and in 1876 a further site was acquired, which became the Carriage & Wagon Works. The original site was devoted to the building and repair of locomotives - Derby Locomotive Works. In 1923 the works came under the control of the London Midland and Scottish Railway (LMS) and in 1948 the British Transport Commission Workshops Division. Then in 1970 British Rail Engineering Limited (BREL) was formed by the British Railways Board, encompassing all BR workshops; this was one of the country's largest engineering concerns. Pictured is the erecting shop in the early 1900s.*

Derby School of Transport. *A rear view, taken in 1954, of the Derby School of Transport designed by W. H. Hamlyn FRIBA for the London Midland & Scottish Railway. The LMS opened the School of Transport at Derby in 1938. It claimed to be the first of its kind in the world providing training and research into modern transport technology, business and marketing. Derby was chosen for the site as it was central to the LMS network and provided easy access to the railway infrastructure for practical training. All the students and tutors needs could be cared for on site.*

DMAG001997 - Picture courtesy of Derby Museums and Art Gallery

DRBY000058 - Picture courtesy of Derby Evening Telegraph

Centenary celebrations at Allen Park Infants School, Allen Street. *In the 1870s Isaac Allen purchased land on either side of the Derby to Swarkestone Road and built a small speculative housing estate. By 1903 there were 150 houses, the Crown Hotel, built in 1891 at a cost of £1,200 and a school on the corner of Allen Street and Poole Street. Initially, the school was under the control of the Alvaston and Boulton School Board and for many years it was used on Sundays for church services. The school celebrated its centenary in March 1980. During the early days the small village settlement was called Allentown. Following further substantial development, Allenton was incorporated into the County Borough of Derby, in 1928.*

DRBY000056 - Picture courtesy of Derby Evening Telegraph

St Edmund's Church, Sinfin Avenue

The fact that St Edmund's Church, seen here in 1980, was only built in 1939 may come as a surprise to some people who may well have considered it much older. Built of Mansfield stone by Eaton of Derby, in Gothic style, it is light and airy with excellent musical acoustics. Across the road, in an attractive, open setting is the War Memorial village, built with the special needs of its disabled occupants in mind. There are over 30 houses, the first being occupied in May 1950. The foundation stone for the village was laid by Princess Elizabeth, before she became Queen, and the Duke of Edinburgh.

DRBY006462 - Picture courtesy of Derby City Council

North front of Osmaston Hall. *Osmaston Hall, pictured c1800 was built for Sir Nicholas Wilmot, between 1696/98 and was lived in by the family, until they moved to Catton Hall. It was then let to the Fox family. During that period, the Royal Agricultural Society held the Royal Show on Osmaston Park in 1843 and 1881. A third show was held there in 1903, when it was attended by Edward VII. In 1888 the Midland Railway bought the house and part of the estate for £90,000. They turned the house into offices, laid a siding almost up to the front door and used the northern part of the park to build the Carriage, Wagon and Locomotive works. The Royal Show was also again held there in 1906, 1921 and 1933.*

Derby Corporation Tram at the Abingdon Street Depot. *The staff at the Abingdon Street Depot standing in front of an open-top tramcar, which has just been fitted with a windscreen at the time of the First World War. Chalked on the window is a war time slogan. This reads: 'Be a sportsman and lend a hand to the lads at the front. They need your help.' After the last tram left, the depot was used as a repair shop for the vehicles, but not for regular maintenance. Following the opening of the Ascot Drive Depot in 1949, all the trolley operations were transferred there, where a large through shed was available. The Abingdon Street Depot closed in 1948 in anticipation of the move, followed some time later, by the closures of Nottingham Road and Osmaston Road Depots.*

DRBY001329 - Picture courtesy of Derby City Council

DMAG001623 - Picture courtesy of Derby Museums and Art Gallery

The Osmaston Road Bus Garage. *Lined up outside the Osmaton Road Garage, c1930 are four Derby Corporation Motor buses that appear to be about to set off on their journeys. From left to right they are No. 27 (CH 8680), a 1929 Guy FCX66 with Short bodywork (withdrawn 1939); No.19 (CH 8337), a 1929 AEC 422 with Brush bodywork (withdrawn 1939); No. 34 (CH 9502), a 1930 Guy FC48 with Brush bodywork (withdrawn 1944); and No. 25 (CH 8343), a 1929 Tilling Stevens B10A2 with locally made Sanderson and Holmes bodywork (withdrawn 1938). Osmaston Road Garage was acquired about 1930, having been previously part of Eastwood & Swinglers Victoria & Railway Ironworks. The garage closed in 1967.*

James Eastwood and Sons, Cotton Lane. *A c1850 picture, which has been taken from an engraving of James Eastwood and Sons, Railway Iron Works, situated off Cotton Lane at Osmaston. The view has been taken looking in a southerly direction, with the Derby-Birmingham railway line in the foreground. The foundry was set up in 1852 by James Eastwood from Chesterfield. Originally he had his foundry built on the Morledge, in the centre of Derby. However, the street was already crowded with cement, colour-grinding, copper and silk works and a decision was quickly made to move to the more spacious site at Cotton Lane.*

DMAG000884 - Picture courtesy of Derby Museums and Art Gallery

DMAG000980 - Picture courtesy of Jesper

Rolls-Royce Motor Works, Nightingale Road. *Rolls-Royce grew from the electrical and mechanical business established by Henry Royce in 1884. Royce built his first motor car in 1904 and in May of that year met Charles Rolls, whose company sold quality cars in London. Henry Royce was a meticulous, self-taught engineer, but he felt more at home designing and improving his cars than he did trying to sell them. He needed an extrovert salesman to convince buyers of the soundness and engineering excellence that he had built into his cars and Charles Stewart Rolls was that type of man. An agreement was reached that Royce Limited would manufacture a range of cars to be exclusively sold by CS Rolls & Co, which would bear the name Rolls-Royce. This led to the formation of what was to become the world famous company, Rolls-Royce and to the launch of the six-cylinder Silver Ghost which, within a year, was hailed as 'the best car in the world'. The original factory was set up in Manchester, but in 1907 it was moved to Derby. The Osmaston Motor Works were built for Rolls-Royce by Andrew Handyside and opened in July 1908. Nightingale Road was built running from Osmaston Road past the works. The Nightingale Road Works are pictured here in 1954.*

DMAG000979 - Picture courtesy of Derby Museums and Art Gallery

Rolls-Royce Motor Works, Nightingale Road. *The interior of the Machine Shop at Rolls-Royce Motor Works on Nightingale Road is pictured c1912. This part of the Machine Shop was used for the manufacture of wheels. All the motor manufacturing business was transferred to Crewe in 1946. The Derby factories were left to concentrate on the design and building of aero engines, which they had begun just prior to the First World War. The first Rolls-Royce aero engine was the Eagle, which was tested in 1915, and by the end of the First World War more than 4,000 Eagle and 2,000 Falcon engines were produced. Rolls-Royce crashed in 1971, due to the escalating research and development costs of the RB211. Fortunately, intervention by the government saved the company and the jobs of the workforce.*

DRBY005895 - Picture courtesy of Derby Evening Telegraph

The first Silver Ghost manufactured by Rolls-Royce. *Up to 1906 Rolls-Royce had built several different models with four- and six-cylinder engines, and even a V-8. For 1907 they decided on a one-model policy for the company. This would permit them to concentrate all efforts on developing it, rather than spreading their resources over several models. The Silver Ghost was that car, which made its debut at the Olympia Motor Show in November, 1906, designated as a 1907 model. To demonstrate the new model's engineering quality, it was taken on a 2,000 mile reliability run, and later completed a 15,000 mile test, with Charles Rolls as one of the drivers. As a result of the testing it broke the world's record for reliability and long distance.*

CHAPTER 11 - DARLEY ABBEY

Only two miles from the centre of Derby, the old village of Darley Abbey is at its most impressive when approached along either side of the River Derwent. The village itself is still full of interest, since the Evans family, between 1782 and 1840, transformed it from a quiet little backwater and it remains an important place in the industrial history of this country.

Few traces remain of Darley Abbey, founded in about 1140, and which later became the richest and most powerful abbey in Derbyshire. The land and properties owned by the abbey covered an extensive area not only in Derbyshire, but also in Nottinghamshire.

Most of the buildings of the once proud monastery were gradually destroyed within two years of the passing of the Act of Dissolution. The only survivors were the building in Darley Street, converted into a public house in 1980, some stonework to houses in Abbey Lane and a burial ground beneath Hill Square.

After the dissolution, life at Darley Abbey continued in a fairly uneventful manner. In the 1730s four mills, a paper mill, a corn mill, a fulling mill and a leather mill all existed here, powered by the Derwent. It was the Industrial Revolution, with water the driving force, which triggered the expansion of what was only a small settlement into an important industrial village.

Thomas Evans, born in 1723 and educated at Cambridge University, was the driving force. He expanded the family business and became a leading industrialist. In 1771, he entered into partnership with Samuel Crompton, who had been mayor of Derby four years earlier, and formed the Crompton and Evans Bank. Both Sir Richard Arkwright and Jedediah Strutt were customers of the bank, which later became known as Thomas Evans and Son, when Samuel Crompton lost interest.

Today Darley Abbey forms part of The Derwent Valley Mills World Heritage Site because of the pioneering work of the Evans family. The old village of Darley Abbey is regarded as a desirable place to live. The mills built by Thomas Evans, on the east bank of the Derwent, remain largely intact although no longer used for cotton spinning, but are still in use for a diverse range of purposes.

Trail: Darley Abbey Park – Darley Street – Boar's Head cotton mills – Folly Road (detour) – West Row – New Road – Brick Row – Church Lane (detour) – Abbey Lane – Mile Ash Lane.

'Darley Hall, the seat of Robert Holden Esquire' 1800s. *The domestic problems of Henry VIII led to the Dissolution of the Monastries, and on the 22 October 1538, the Abbot of Darley was forced to hand the abbey over to the Royal Commission. The abbey was gradually destroyed and the chattels sold. Two years later the site and property surrounding it was granted to Sir William West. A house was built on the hillside sometime later. It changed hands several times before William Woolley, rebuilt the house in brick in 1727. The estate next became the property of Mr. Heath, a banker in Derby, who leased the hall to the Holden family, who bought the freehold on Heath's bankruptcy.*

DRBY005308 - Picture courtesy of Derby City Council

DRBY005076 - Picture courtesy of Derby City Council

Darley Hall. *In 1777 Joseph Pickford extended the house for Robert Holden. The hall remained in the possession of the Holden family until 1835, when it was purchased by Samuel Evans, Thomas's grandson, who was given short term financial assistance by his cousin, Walter Evans. It was a complicated transaction as any transfer of ownership of the estate had to be approved by a Special Act of Parliament. Once everything had been completed, the Evans family moved from their previous home at Darley House. The hall remained in the ownership of the family, until the death of Ada Evans in 1929, although their interests in the cotton mills at Darley Abbey had ended 26 years previously with the death of Walter Evans. The picture of the ivy clad hall was taken in 1894.*

The drawing room at Darley Hall. *The Evans family lived at the hall for approaching 100 years, this picture of the drawing room having been taken a few years before the death of Walter Evans. Apart from Darley Hall Estate, the family also acquired the Little Chester Estate in 1875 from the Ecclesiastical Commissioners for England, the land being controlled by the Duke of Devonshire. It lay on the opposite side of the River Derwent and consisted of 76 acres and included the site of the Roman fort of Derventio. The wide open space to the north of Little Chester is now used for recreational facilities.*

DRBY004672 - Picture courtesy of Derby City Council

DMAG001760 - Picture courtesy of Derby Museums and Art Gallery

Darley Hall and Darley Abbey Park. *This is a copy of a Valentine's postcard, which dates back to the early 1900s, when Ada Evans, the widow of Walter Evans, lived at Darley Hall. In the picture her gardener is mowing the lawns in the park, which was landscaped by William Evans and had attractive flower beds, shrubberies and lawns running down to the River Derwent. Following the death of Ada Evans in 1929, Derby Corporation took over the house and grounds. The hall was converted for the use of Derby Central School, until 1958, when the school moved to a new building on Breadsall Hill Top. Darley Hall was demolished in 1962, when no further use for the building could be found, apart from the billiard room, which is now the Terrace Café. Under the archway at the rear is the former Stable Yard, at the time of writing, surrounded by buildings in a poor state of repair.*

Darley Church and Darley House. *A delightful, 1893, colour tinted postcard, postmarked 5 May 1905. The picture shows the weir, Darley House and St Matthew's Church. The church was completed in 1819 and financed by the Evans family. Darley House was built for Walter Evans around 1785 and overlooked both the mills and the village. The house was positioned on the hillside between what is now Spinney Close and Weirdale Road. A row of fruit trees was grown between the house and the mill to soften the view. In 1835, the Evans family moved to Darley Hall and Darley House was finally demolished in 1932. The gate-keeper's lodge on the corner of Brick Row still remains as a reminder.*

DMAG300170 - Picture courtesy of Derby Museums and Art Gallery

Darley Abbey (Shown after conversion for use as cottages) c1850s. *The only remaining building from the original abbey is the old Abbey building in Darley Street, which was partitioned for cottages in the 19th century. Later it fell into disrepair and was in the danger of demolition, only to be rescued in 1980, when it was converted into a public house. The pub is on two floors, and is well worth a visit to look around and enjoy the hospitality. Although its original use is uncertain, it may well once have been used by the monks to entertain guests. During the renovation 12th century pottery was unearthed. Some of the stonework in Abbey Lane is also thought to date back to the former abbey.*

DRBY005306 - Picture courtesy of Derby City Council

Weir on River Derwent, Darley Abbey. *The weir runs diagonally across the river for 360 feet, including a small island. It starts on the east bank at a point just below the bridge, which was constructed to provide access for the mill workers and visitors and finishes on the village side of the Derwent. Water was channelled into the wheelhouse, turning the waterwheel, its speed controlled by the use of the sluice gates to manage the volume of water. A series of drive shafts on each floor, connected by a belt, were driven by the waterwheel. The original system was gradually modified and extended and in 1896 was replaced by turbines and by electricity just over 70 years later.*

DCHQ003833 - Picture courtesy of Brighouse Collection

DRBY004942 - Picture courtesy of Derby Evening Telegraph

Darley Abbey Raft Race. *New Year's Day events on the River Derwent are quite common and an annual raft race also takes place at Matlock Bath. This picture was taken on the 1st January 1982, with spectators getting a close up view of all the activity in the river. The river has a truly remarkable tale to tell. Although only 60 miles in length, it fills great reservoirs near its source, and has been harnessed to power mills. Most important of all, it played an outstanding part in the Industrial Revolution. On its journey the river flows through parkland past Chatsworth, and later through the narrow gorge at Matlock, before flowing through meadows and the busy city of Derby on its way to a meeting with the River Trent. The existence of the river was the reason that Thomas Evans set up business at Darley Abbey, where mills may have existed for nearly 1,000 years.*

View of River Derwent showing Darley Abbey Mills, Hall and Church. *Following the building of Long Mill, the mill works were continuously expanded well into the 1900s. The invention of the sewing machine in 1846 gave a considerable boost to the industry. The raw cotton arrived at the ports of London, Liverpool and Hull and was transported using inland waterways to its destination. Derby Canal completed in 1796, was a very important factor in the success of the mill operation and Walter Evans was appointed treasurer of Derby Canal Company. As the canal did not quite reach Darley Abbey Mills, to avoid the weir at Derby, a short branch canal, called the Phoenix, was built. It had two locks, the White Bear Lock and the Phoenix Lock. This splendid picture was taken in the early 1880s.*

DRBY001581 - Picture courtesy of Richard Keene Ltd

DRBY004961 - Picture courtesy of Derby City Council

Boar's Head Cotton Mills complex. *Founded by Thomas Evans, it was one of the most important industrial enterprises in an age of great innovation and progress. The boar's head trademark, taken from the crest of the family coat-of-arms, was used by Evans to market his thread. It achieved recognition in the many parts of the world where he traded, as a symbol of quality. Awards were won at the London Exhibitions of 1861 and 1862 as well as exhibitions in Dublin and Paris in later years. The earlier mills were built on the south side of the road running through the complex as indicated by the hatched area on the aerial photograph.*

Darley Abbey Mills. *Originally the mills were water powered, the chimney marking a later stage with the arrival of steam. At the outset to ensure an adequate volume of water to drive the waterwheel and increase the speed with which the machinery was turned, it was necessary to increase the depth of the Derwent. The river was dredged regularly from Allestree Ford, the sediment was of good quality and the sand extracted was found suitable for building. Derby Corporation also discovered the sand was ideal for sanding tram lines in bad weather. As you walk through the mill complex, the route used to channel the water into the wheelhouse is indicated by the two low walls, which once formed a bridge.*

DMAG000866 - Picture courtesy of Mark Higginson

DMAG000850 - Picture courtesy of Derby Museums and Art Gallery

Boar's Head Cotton Mills. *This picture was taken c1900 and shows a group of women workers, inside the canteen at Boar's Head Cotton Mill. The women are obviously posing for the photograph, and it is interesting to note how light and roomy the canteen appears. In 1903 the Evans family sold the mills. The paper mill on the west side of the river was demolished in 1934, but all the main buildings on the east side remain. They are now used by numerous small businesses, with Darleys Restaurant overlooking the weir. The buildings as a group are an important part of The Derwent Valley Mills World Heritage Site.*

Boar's Head Mills 'Spool or Reel Turning Machines'. *In this 1862 picture male workers are using Spool or Reel Turning machines, to make cotton bobbins. By the early 1820s, following the additions of the Middle Mill (1804/5), East Mill (1811) and West Mill (1821) the mills employed over five hundred people. In addition there were various other ancillary buildings, where reeling, dyeing and glazing took place. The long low building on the north side of the road between the mills was the gassing shed, where stray fibres were burnt off cotton thread by passing through a gas flame at high speed. The tall chimney was part of the former engine house.*

DRBY004965 - Picture courtesy of Derby City Council

Boar's Head Mills Cotton Winding Machine. *Women workers are seen here, in 1862, winding cotton onto bobbins using machines at the Boar's Head cotton mills. In the mid 1800s work started at 6am during the week, the mill bell having rang three quarters of an hour previously to arouse the workers from their slumbers, with a further bell half an hour later indicating it was time to set off for the walk to the mill. At 8.30am, half an hour was taken for breakfast and, at 1pm, an hour was allowed for lunch. The working day finished at 5.30pm. Saturday working was restricted to a maximum of nine hours.*

DRBY004967 - Picture courtesy of Derby City Council

Derbyshire's last working Toll Bar, Darley Abbey Mills. *The Gate House, pictured in the 1980s is situated where the mill site is entered across the River Derwent. It was used to control the number of people entering the site, raw materials arriving and finished goods departing. In more recent times it has seen service as a toll bar and in the picture a Mrs Wood is seen on the left. The building opposite is the West Mill, which was constructed using cast iron to help avoid the risk of fire, the protection of which the Long Mill did not have when it was burnt down 32 years earlier. In order to achieve the right balance a number of windows have actually been painted on the wall.*

DCAV000583 - Picture courtesy of Derbyshire County Council

Bridge over the brook near Folly House. *Folly House and bridge, pictured in the 1940s, are located on the eastern side of the River Derwent at the end of Folly Road. It is now part of the Darley Abbey Conservation Area. The building is said to have been built as a mill, but because of the weirs upstream, there was not enough power to drive the mill, hence its unfortunate name. It was sold to the Evans family who converted it into three houses, one of which was later demolished. The wooden bridge was replaced in 1948, but due to problems of erosion, a new steel footbridge supported by piled foundations was recently put in place.*

DRBY003651 - Picture courtesy of Derby City Council

DRBY003387 - Picture courtesy of Derby City Council

Cottages built for workers at Evans' Mills at West Row. *All industrial development required a substantial labour force and the Evans family set about the task of acquiring and maintaining sufficient people to meet the growing demand for labour. This was no easy task as many framework knitters blamed the factory system for taking away their livelihood and independence. There was also a suspicion about the working conditions in factories. Generous inducements were offered to potential workers in the form of above average wages and new well-built brick-houses, together with a parcel of land and a cow. At the Old Road end of West Row, pictured in c1970s, the single storey buildings facing the terraced cottages were once used as privies.*

Darley Abbey former school, Brick Row. *Thomas Evans founded a Sunday school in 1794, in a room in the roof of Long Mill. In 1826, St Matthew's School a purpose built building was opened in Brick Row. It was very advanced in design for its time, with spacious airy well lit rooms and high ceilings. A fine clock was set in the centre of the front wall. The Schoolmaster was accommodated in an apartment on the left wing of the school and the Schoolmistress at the other end. It was the Schoolmaster who had much the largest quarters, presumably because it was expected he would have a family to house and his colleague would be a spinster. This view was taken in 1978.*

DRBY000100 - Picture courtesy of Derby Evening Telegraph

DRBY001580 - Picture courtesy of Don Farnsworth

Brick Row. *Thomas Evans soon realised that he would have to attract workers to the mill, Darley Abbey at that time only having a very small population. To do this he set about building houses and providing other amenities. From about 1790, well built terraces were erected composed of mainly three storey dwellings. By 1811, Flat Square, Hill Square, upper Mile Ash Lane and Brick Row had been built. A few years later a school was built at the New Road end of Brick Row, and it would appear the children, seen in this c1900 picture, are on their way to school watched by their families.*

St Matthew's Church, Church Lane. *This c1860 picture is of St Matthew's Church, which was built by Moses Wood of Nottingham. It was consecrated in 1819 and endowed by Walter Evans as was the village school, which opened six years later. Nine members of the Evans family are buried in the crypt. Prior to the opening of the church, for the 280 years following the dissolution of the monastery at Darley Abbey, the local community had to travel to St Alkmond's in Derby for Sunday worship. The iron gates to the church are particularly impressive, one bearing the coat of arms of St Matthew and the other the Diocese of Derby under whose authority it comes.*

DRBY005310 - Picture courtesy of Derby City Council

DRBY004670 - Picture courtesy of Derby City Council

Stone coffin, St Matthew's Church, Church Lane. *This c1900 picture shows a stone coffin found in Darley Abbey village during excavations. It was removed to Nut Wood (where this view was taken) and later placed in St Matthew's churchyard. The lid has been lost and its original site is not known. It has been chiselled out of a block of stone, is quite small and was possibly made for the burial of a child. Close to the coffin, in front of the St Matthew's Church Fellowship Room are a large number of slate tablets identifying workers' from the Evans' estate who are buried in the churchyard. It was the practice of the Evans family to pay for the burials of employees.*

Abbey Lane. *Abbey Lane, pictured in 1978, follows on from Mile Ash Lane, where the houses built by the Evans family end with a row of two storey terraced cottages and finally, Elm Cottage. The cottage is a detached building that was once used as an Estate Office. The name changes again to Church Lane at the junction with Old Lane. Much of Abbey Lane pre-dates the Evans house building era, and the old house in the picture may well have been constructed using stone from the former abbey. The cottages opposite were in place before the main village expansion took place. Formerly known by the locals as 'Shop Lane', where a shop still remains.*

DRBY005080 - Picture courtesy of Derby Evening Telegraph

The Four House Cluster. *Located at the junction of Mile Ash Lane and Lavender Row, it consists of four individual houses built together as a free standing group, known as a Cluster House. Built in 1792, it is reputedly the oldest known example of this type of dwelling in existence. Two more recent white two-storey cluster houses are to be found on New Road, facing where the mill workers allotments used to be sited, now the home of the Methodist Church. On the same side, near the bottom of New Road, are two further three-storey cluster houses. Lavender Row can be seen to the left of the picture.*

The Village Lock-Up. *At the southern entrance to Darley Abbey near the road leading up Darley Grove from Derby, outside the Hall Gates in New Street was a lock-up, seen here in 1954. It was the watchman's duty to arrest those under the influence of drink and to lock them away and note the names of all the girls returning after 10pm. Many of the young ladies avoided this by hoisting their long skirts over their heads and running away as fast as they were able. It was demolished in 1954. The gardens on the top side of the path leading into the park are particularly noteworthy as they house part of the National Hydrangea and Viburnum Collection.*

DRBY000136 - Picture courtesy of Derby City Council

Turnpike Toll House and Post Office, Duffield Road. *The toll-house seen here c1920, now demolished, is decorated with the distinctive bargeboards and gables of the Victorian period. Turnpike Trusts, originally set up in 1706 and extended in 1735, were not popular as they required people to pay to travel on roads, which had previously been free to use. Under the Turnpike Act the trustees could build new roads or assume responsibility for existing roads. To finance their projects, a trust was allowed to collect a fee from every traveller using one of its roads. This caused riots and some toll-gates and houses were destroyed as a result. However, Turnpike Trusts were a success, and the money raised was used in part to finance the building of new and better roads. At the time this picture was taken the premises were being used as a shop.*

DRBY004960 - Picture courtesy of Derby City Council

CHAPTER 12 - LITTLE CHESTER

Little Chester, or Chester Green as it is more commonly known, was once the site of a Roman town. It may well have been inhabited before the Romans arrived; fragments of Iron Age pottery have been found in the area. As Derby's oldest suburb, some of its thoroughfares are also almost 2,000 years old.

Today, Little Chester continues to flourish and became a Conservation Area in 1993. Highly regarded as an excellent place to live, it is within easy walking distance of Derby City Centre and is well endowed with open spaces and leisure facilities. Originally it included Derby Racecourse and all the land up to Beaufort Street and Old Mansfield Road in the east, Nottingham Road in the south, the Derwent on the west and Darley and Little Eaton in the north.

Established in the latter part of the first century by the Romans, the military role of this vital river-crossing was diminished as a prosperous small town emerged. By the beginning of the fifth century, commercial activity appears to have stopped. But it is unclear how long the walls remained, giving protection for the native Romano-British population. Eventually the settlement was probably abandoned for a time, but was refortified in 874 by the Norsemen.

The Romans set up a fort in about AD50 at Strutt's Park, to protect the river crossing on the western side of the Derwent. Originally it was thought they remained there for about 30 years, before establishing a large new fortified settlement across the river at Little Chester, which they called Derventio. In the light of recent finds, historians have revised their estimate and think the Romans probably remained at Strutt's Park for a much longer period.

Little remains at Little Chester today, apart from two Roman wells, one on Marcus Street and the other in the garden of the vicarage of St Paul's Church. However, a series of excavations in the last fifty years has established both its importance and prosperity, including the discovery of an underfloor heating system on Parker's Piece and an abundance of coins.

The Roman occupation did not limit itself solely to the fort at Derventio and the area directly outside. Recent excavations have revealed the existence of an industrial site and burial ground on the edge of the Old Derby Racecourse and other scattered finds, including a farm at Willington.

In more recent times the arrival of the railway had a considerable impact on Little Chester. On the eastern side of Mansfield Road and bounded by Fox Street, the Midland Railway erected a huge complex of sidings and warehouses at St Mary's Wharf. The line from Friargate Station to Ilkeston severed the north and western parts of the suburb. Little evidence of the line remains after the embankment was removed in 1968, apart from Andrew Handyside's bridge over the Derwent.

Trail: St Mary's Bridge – Mansfield Road – Chester Green – Mansfield Road – Old Chester Road – Chester Green Road – Marcus Street – Handyside's Bridge – City Road – Mansfield Street.

DRBY000850 - Picture courtesy of Derby City Council

Artefacts excavated at the Chester Green Site. *Some of the finds put on display in Derby Museum from Sherwin's excavations on Parker's Piece in 1926. Charles Bakewell Sherwin was the Borough Surveyor and he was employed, together with his workforce, to level and prepare the ground at Little Chester for recreational facilities. The land having been recently conveyed to Derby Borough from the estate of Ada Evans of Darley Abbey, and was at that time farmland. This area is now known as Darley Playing Fields. As Sherwin's workforce carried out their excavation works, the line of Ryknield Street was found running north through the fields towards Breadsall. Artefacts dating back to the Roman occupation of the site were also discovered.*

Bridge Inn, on the corner of Mansfield Road and St Mary's Bridge. *Originally a private house, the inn was established about 60 years after the property was built in the 1790s. However, it may well have been in use as a pub prior to that, operating under another name. It was always popular on Derby Regatta Days and once had a boat house of its own. At one time a room on the south side of the premises, with access from the bridge, was used for various trades, including greengrocery and a café. For many years an old penny–farthing bike was fixed to the top of the wall near the rear entrance.*

DRBY002841 - Picture courtesy of Derby City Council

Houses on the west side of Mansfield Road. *Mansfield Road has been one of the main transport routes leading to and from Derby since the days when the road first became suitable for vehicular transport. In the mid-eighteenth century, it was one of eight routes into Derby from the north east with a turnpike situated at the junction between Mansfield and Alfreton Roads. The first form of public transport to serve Little Chester was a horse drawn bus, where passengers sat facing each other on either side of the bus. During the First World War, this form of transport ended and was succeeded by an experimental battery powered vehicle known locally as 'The Tank'. In 1924, this gave way to the petrol engine.*

DMAG200600 - Picture courtesy of Derby Museums and Art Gallery

DRBY000361 - Picture courtesy of Derby Evening Telegraph

***The Duke of Clarence Inn on Mansfield** Road. This picture was taken in 1981, with St Paul's Church just visible in the background. The pub originally occupied only half of the building and was later extended into the adjoining house. It was named after Admiral HRH Prince William, 1st Duke of Clarence and St Andrew's (1765-1837). He was the third son of George III who eventually succeeded as King William IV. Following the accession it was briefly known as William IV, before reverting to its original name.*

***Derby Rail Freight Depot, also known as St Mary's Freight Yard, Mansfield Road.** Less than 10 years after it opened, Derby Railway Station became very congested and goods trains in particular experienced long delays. In order to help rectify this situation a large goods station was built adjacent to St Mary's Bridge where an extensive wharf was established. The goods branch opened 1855 and a few years later more land was acquired and the facilities expanded. The station complex has been built over in recent years; one of its new occupiers is the St Mary's Wharf Police Station. A few of the old railway buildings still remain now put to different uses. The freight depot is pictured in 1986.*

DRBY000460 - Picture courtesy of Derby Evening Telegraph

DRBY002621 - Picture courtesy of Derby City Council

War memorial, next to St Paul's Church, Mansfield Road. *The First World War Memorial Cross, pictured c1970, is in the centre of a walled semi-circular recess. The two granite tablets to the low boundary wall, on either side of the Cross, list the names of the fallen during the Second World War. One tablet is inscribed 'Keep in Remembrance the Men from this Parish whose names are recorded here. They gave their lives that Justice and Freedom, mercy and love should survive'. The other recorded the years '1939-1945' and the 26 names of 'The Fallen', the lettering similar to that of the First World War Memorial Cross.*

DRBY000716 - Picture courtesy of Derby Evening Telegraph

First World War Memorial Plaque, St Mary's Goods Yard. *The memorial commemorates the 22 workers at St Mary's Railway Goods Wharf who enlisted and died in action during the 1914-18 War. It was originally placed on the side of a building, which stood just inside the main entrance of the yard. It is now located on platform one at Derby Railway Station. St Paul's Church holds a leather bound volume of remembrance, donated to the parish in 1935 by Mr and Mrs Leonard Walker. The 'Book of Remembrance' lists all 934 parishioners who saw action and the names of those who died are still read out on Armistice Sunday. The picture was taken in 1986.*

DRBY001636 - Picture courtesy of Derby City Council

The New Parish Church of St Paul's, Mansfield Road. *By the mid-1800s the population of Little Chester had grown considerably to over 500 people. To meet a growing need St Paul's Church was built. It was constructed mainly of Little Eaton Quarry Stone and is now a Grade II listed building along with the War Memorial, which is classed as an ancient monument. The script under the hand tinted lithograph of c1850 reads:-'Day and Son lithographers to the Queen. This print of the New Parish Church of St Paul, Derby (erected in memory of the Right Reverend Walter Augustus Shirley D D. Lord Bishop of Sodor and Man, sometime Archdeacon of Derby.) is with permission dedicated to the Right Reverend the Lord Bishop of Lichfield by his Lordship's most obedient servants, Barry and Brown, Architects'. The church was consecrated on 22 May 1850. At first it was a chapel associated with St Alkmund's and replaced a mission room on City Road. During the First World War troops were encamped around Little Chester and the Racecourse. Each Sunday morning they were marched along Mansfield Road to St Paul's for a Church Parade at 9.30am. The custom was to brighten up the march by singing a marching song. However, when the Vicar heard them singing a ribald song to a well known hymn tune, he not unnaturally raised strong objections. One was 'We are Lord Kitchener's Army' to the tune of 'Aurelia'.*

Little Chester Heritage Centre, which opened in September 2001, is located at the church. For anyone interested in the local history of Derby, its industry and the Roman Empire, a visit to the centre is essential. It is normally open on Sunday afternoons from Easter to October.

DMAG200590 - Picture courtesy of Derby Museums and Art Gallery

Chester Green. *Chester Green, seen here in 1990, has been in existence as an area of open space since the Middle Ages. In the past it was a rough place and some families would not let their children go near it, although others used it for sport and recreation as well as occasional meetings. One of the problems was it was poorly drained and regularly flooded. However, following the incorporation of Little Chester into Derby Borough, in 1877, the scheme to lay a new green was approved. On the 4 November 1882 the first turf was cut, but the work took several years to complete. After that the green soon became an important venue for sport and celebrations.*

An 1893 view of the Coach and Horses Inn on the corner of Mansfield Road and Old Chester Road. *The inn has been in existence since at least the time William Stukeley drew a map of Little Chester in 1719, when it was called 'The Crown'. In the mid-1750s, the name was changed to the Coach and Horses, as the road that ran past the pub became a coaching route and coaches started using its facilities. It was then a low brick building with a thatched roof and may have been timber-framed. Around 1905 the inn was rebuilt in its present style. A bowling green was added on the south side, this was overlooked by a verandah from which patrons could watch the games. The green is now a car park. An extension was added in 1981. One well known landlord, Charles Radford who kept the pub from 1916 until he retired in 1949, started to keep small animals in the 1920s. His 'Pets Corner' included three monkeys, six rabbits, ducks, geese and over 100 birds including parrots and a magpie.*

DMAG300194 - Picture courtesy of Derby Museums and Art Gallery

DMAG200610 - Picture courtesy of Derby Museums and Art Gallery

School Farm or Stone House Prebend, Old Chester Road. *Stone House Prebend, pictured in 1990 was also known as School Farm. It is located at the end of Old Chester Road facing the River Derwent. Formerly it was a timber framed building, the income from the farm supporting the canons of the College of All Saints' until 1549. It is probably the oldest domestic property in Derby. Parts of the building are medieval, including a huge exterior chimney breast; the remainder is late 16th to early 17th century. On the opposite side of the road stands Derwent House, a 17th century farmhouse, where traces have been found of an earlier great hall. It is now a private residence, the outbuildings forming part of Little Chester's recreational facilities.*

Chester Green Road. *The housing boom in Little Chester, Derby's first suburb, took off in the 1890s, when houses were built in a semi-crescent formation, along Chester Green Road seen here in the 1980s. They were built to a good standard, with long back gardens running down to the Great Northern Railway line, with room for a shed and perhaps a workshop or greenhouse. Marcus Street leads off Chester Green Road, where the remains of an old Roman Well are to be found. Much of the iron fencing around the Green was taken for salvage for the Second World War effort.*

DRBY006545 - Picture courtesy of Derby Evening Telegraph

Well Dressing, Marcus Street. *In 1968, some of the remains of the Roman settlement called Derventio were revealed, following the removal of the railway and embankment. Two wells were discovered and the one at the end of Marcus Street, the Local Authority decided should be preserved, together with a number of post holes which had also been discovered. An experienced well dresser, Derek Palmer, from Chaddesden was enlisted to lead the team of dressers and the Marcus Street Well was dressed for the first time in 1980. A year later permission was obtained to dress the well in the Vicarage Garden. The 1988 Marcus Street Well Dressing is shown in this picture.*

DRBY005556 - Picture courtesy of Derby Evening Telegraph

Chester Green Well Dressings. *The ladies in this 1982 picture are in the early stages of petalling, which requires considerable skill and patience in creating the final product. Well dressing is extremely hard, but satisfying work. It takes a team of volunteers many hours, from gathering berries, mosses, flowers and all the other essential materials required to complete the design, to the erection of the boards at the chosen site. Well dressing is not quite unique to Derbyshire, but it is the county where the tradition is the strongest. Almost all the wells dressed every year are either within the county, or only a short distance from its boundary. The event at Chester Green used to take place during the Spring Bank Holiday and was followed by a procession to each well for the Act of Dedication. Recently the event has not been held every year.*

DRBY002483 - Picture courtesy of Derby Evening Telegraph

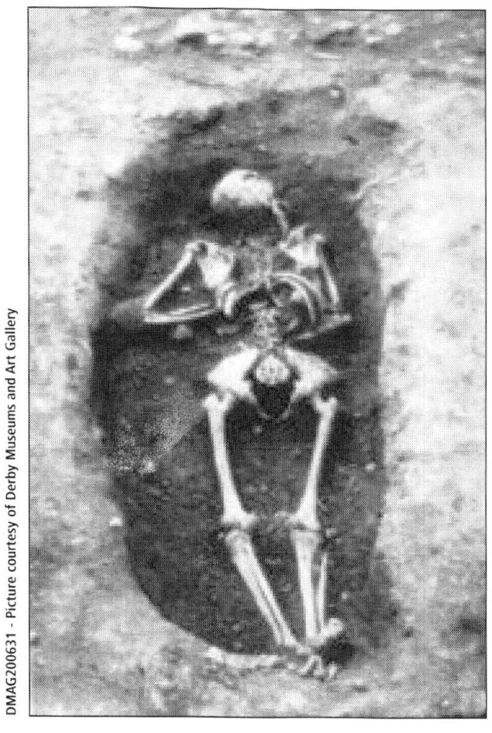

DMAG200631 - Picture courtesy of Derby Museums and Art Gallery

Little Chester excavations. *The archaeological excavations at Little Chester during 1971/2, revealed a number of sixth and early seventh century graves, which were found at the junction of Marcus Street and Old Chester Road. In one of the graves lay the skeleton of a young girl, who had been buried fully clothed, but all that remained was her jewellery and garment fastenings. In some of the men's graves, their weapons had been placed next to them. The excavation also uncovered part of the original Roman wall. There are several descriptive information boards strategically located around Little Chester that tell the story of the Roman occupation.*

Former Railway Bridge over River Derwent – Handyside's Bridge. *Situated behind Haslam's old factory on City Road is the fine bowstring bridge built by Andrew Handyside in 1877, which crosses the Derwent. Handyside established his Britannia heavy engineering works and iron foundry in 1848 and although he originally produced ornamental and architectural ironwork, he later became involved with railway architecture. The bridge formerly carried the Great Northern Railway's Nottingham to Derby line between North Parade and City Road, and remained in use until closed by Dr Beeching. There was originally a public footway along the near side of the structure, but this was later removed, when the bridge was renovated. Since then, pedestrians have used the main span, walking where the tracks were once laid.*

DMAG001965 - Picture courtesy of Derby Museums and Art Gallery

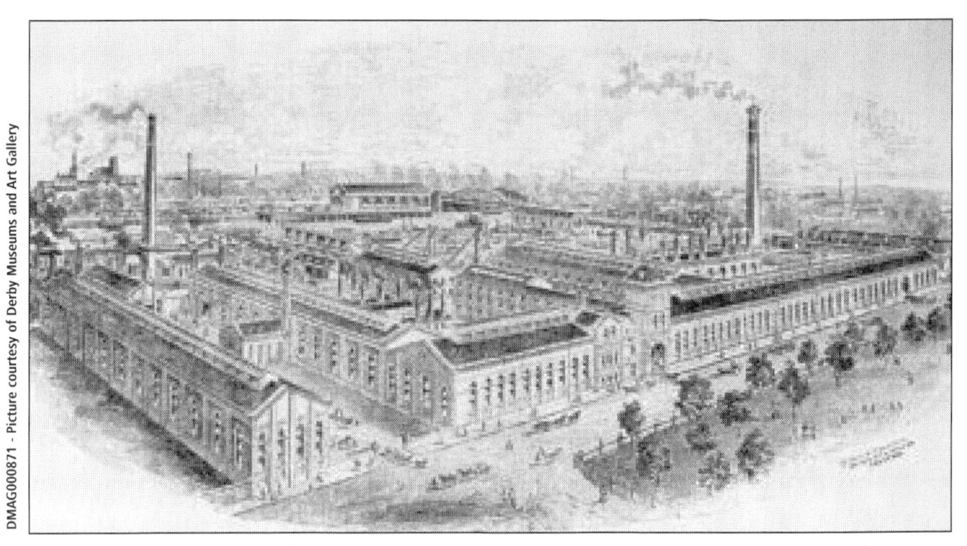

DMAG000871 - Picture courtesy of Derby Museums and Art Gallery

The Union Foundry, City Road. *This c1890 engraving is a slightly exaggerated depiction of the Haslam Foundry and Engineering Company's Union Foundry, on City Road, Little Chester. City Road can be seen in the foreground and the River Derwent is visible in the distance. The Great Northern Railway's line runs across the top of the picture with the same companies Duke Street Goods Yard detectable on the far bank of the Derwent. Haslam's Foundry was established in the 1860s by Alfred Haslam, whose father William was a whitesmith and bell hanger of St Peter's Street. The company was initially engaged in heavy engineering, but later specialised in the manufacture of refrigeration equipment.*

Haslam and Company Refrigeration Unit, City Road. *This picture c1915-20 shows the interior of one of Haslam's refrigeration units at the Union Foundry in Little Chester. Haslam changed from heavy engineering and boiler making to win the race to provide the first commercial dry air plant for ships, enabling frozen meat to be imported long distances. The first ship to have the plant installed was SS Cuzco which brought back 17,000 lamb carcasses from Australia, enabling his firm to monopolise the business until 1894. Haslam also supplied many land based operations with refrigeration units, including docks, hospitals and hotels. In 1891 he employed 650 people, almost all of whom worked at his Little Chester head quarters.*

DMAG000954 - Picture courtesy of Derby Museums and Art Gallery

DMAG000872 - Picture courtesy of Derby Museums and Art Gallery

Haslam and Newton Ltd, City Road Works. *This aerial view shows the City Road Works of Haslam and Newton Limited and dates back to 1930. It was formerly the Union Foundry of the Haslam Foundry and Engineering Company. City Road runs across the picture horizontally from right to left, with Chester Green beyond. The London and North Eastern Railway Line from Nottingham to Friargate Station crosses at an angle from the left to go over the River Derwent. The same companies Duke Street goods yard occupies the riverside in the foreground. The large building in the bottom corner of the photograph is Bath Street Mills, a former elastic web factory.*

DCHQ001428 - Picture courtesy of Derbyshire County Council

E W Bliss Ltd. Works. *Pictured in the mid-1900s are a group of workers in the factory - back row, left to right, are Charlie Bolton, Roy (?), Jack Bentley and Jack Morton. On the front row are Frank (?), four unnamed workers, then Bill Ashworth and Frank Marshall. The works closed in 2004, by which time its name had changed to Aida Bliss.*

DMAG000869 - Picture courtesy of Derby Museums and Art Gallery

E W Bliss (England) Ltd Works, City Road. *This c1950s picture shows the front of the Bliss Works, which were formerly the Haslam Foundry and Engineering Company's Union Foundry. The American-founded firm, E W Bliss (England) Ltd manufactured tins and cans, and later hydraulic presses. They came to England in 1906 and moved to Derby in 1939/40. This photograph is taken looking north along City Road from the junction with St Paul's Road. A lorry belonging to the company (Reg. RC 8223) is parked outside the main entrance. This twin gabled section was subsequently rebuilt in a more modern style.*

DMAG000977 - Picture courtesy of Derby Museums and Art Gallery

Platers and Stampers Ltd, City Road. *A group of workers photographed in 1949, during their morning break at the Platers and Stampers Factory in Little Chester. The factory made pressure cookers, which were invented in 1679 by a French Physicist called Denis Papin. His steam digester - pressure cooker, was a closed vessel with a tightly fitting lid that confined the steam at a higher pressure, considerably raising the boiling point of the water. This airtight cooker, cooked food quicker than traditional methods, and at the same time preserved the nutrients. A safety valve of Papin's making prevented explosions. The pressure cooker became a very popular addition to British kitchens, and is still used today.*

Mansfield Street Methodist Chapel. *The chapel celebrated its 100th birthday on 25 October 1987, when a special Centenary Service was led by the Rev. Dr. RJ Taylor of Westminster Central Hall. A book written by the Minister, the Rev. David Hall was published, recording the story of the church and naming the members who had faithfully worshipped there over the last 100 years. Arthur Thomas Barlow was particularly notable, as after he had undergone treatment at the Derbyshire Royal Infirmary, he was so appreciative of the care provided, he worked tirelessly for the rest of his life arranging concerts to raise funds for the hospital. Gracie Fields featured in one concert and he even persuaded a member of the Royal family to act as a Patron.*

DMAG200594 - Picture courtesy of Derby Museums and Art Gallery

CHAPTER 13 - LITTLEOVER AND MICKLEOVER

LITTLEOVER

From Anglo Saxon times, if not before, a small village existed at Littleover. Rykneld Street, the Old Roman Road, passes through Littleover and it is possible a settlement was set up near the road. The old village centre lay just off the main road close to the church. But as Derby expanded and the green fields separating the two became less, a battle to integrate Littleover into Derby commenced.

It was only in 1866 that Littleover became a separate parish from Mickleover, Findern and Potlock, but it was not long before its newly created independence came under threat. The arrival of the railway and industrialisation was producing rapid expansion of the population in Derby, and the Borough Council began to cast an acquisitive eye towards the village. Already the chiefs of industry were starting to move out of the over crowded town into the country and some built their houses in Littleover.

In 1890 a small part of the parish was transferred to St Werburgh's in Derby and the battle for Littleover began. The Derby Improvement Act of 1901 sought to take part of the village into the Borough and divide the rest of the parish between Findern and Mickleover. This proposal was defeated with the help of Colonel Gascoyne of Fairfield House, who spent over one thousand pounds of his own money to back the village's stand for independence.

Apart from the building of a few large houses and parks, little expansion took place in the village, until the Derby Tramway network was extended in 1908 to the parish boundary at Littleover Lodge. This presented the opportunity for the less well off to live in the country and commute to work. Twenty-five years later when the trams were replaced by trolley buses the route was extended through the village to Chain Lane.

In 1928 a part of the parish was absorbed by Derby and this enabled the Borough Council to construct the Ring Road through what had been the northern part of the parish. But in 1947 when a referendum was held, Littleover residents voted overwhelmingly to retain their independent status.

However, as Derby and Littleover continued to expand, the inevitable occurred and in 1968, the parish was absorbed into the Borough. By this time Littleover had been developed considerably by the sale of the land from The Grange and Pastures estates.

Although Littleover is now a suburb of Derby, despite its size many local people still refer to it as 'the village.' To add credibility to this, the fish and chip shop and until recently a food store proudly displayed the word 'Village' on their fascia boards. The expansive development on the south western side of Littleover goes one better and is known as Heatherton Village.

Trail: Normanton Lane – Shepherd Street – Church Street – The Hollow – Hillsway – Burton Road – Pastures Hill.

Normanton Lane. *By 1931, the population of Littleover had increased substantially as the surrounding farmland was gradually taken over for development. The former parkland of the once isolated country houses of The Grange, Littleover House and the Old Hall disappeared to be replaced by villas similar to those in Normanton Lane, seen here in this c1930 picture. The Vicarage which stood near the top of the lane was demolished in 1963 and bungalows erected in its place. The new development being aptly named Old Vicarage Close.*

DMAG001084 - Picture courtesy of Derby Museums and Art Gallery

DRBY007761 - Picture courtesy of Derby City Council

Old Cottages on Shepherd Street. *Shepherd Street was originally known as Dark Lane, with high banks and overhanging trees alongside what was a narrow, steep lane. It was cleared and widened in the 19th century, by a Mr Sheppard and was renamed after him, although the spelling appears to have altered slightly. The Co-operative Society opened its first store in the village, on the corner of Burton Road, where the Derbyshire Building Society (Nationwide) branch is now located. The Methodist Chapel built in 1867, used to stand on the opposite corner. Further down the street the 19th century White Swan is still open for business, in past summers a blaze of colour with hanging baskets and tubs.*

Staff at St Peter's School, Church of England School, Church Street. *Pictured here in 1958 (left to right) are (back row) Mr M Stanton, Mr L Crozier, Mr G Nash (Deputy Head), Mr T Whitehall (Head), Mr J Williams, Mr J Grundy, (front row) Mrs Keene (secretary), Mrs P Marriott, Mrs Brown, Mrs S Burton, Miss A Parker and Mrs E Blunt. St Peter's Church School was built in 1846 and made provision for 110 boys and girls and 50 infants. Prior to the opening of the new school, education had been the responsibility of the church and a Dame School run in a private house.*

DRBY007471 - Picture courtesy of Derby City Council

St Peter's Church, Littleover. *The first church to be erected in the village was possibly a wooden structure and preceded the Norman Conquest, although there is no mention of it in the Domesday Book. The present church still retains a Norman doorway and font. The windows of the church were replaced in the 14th century, and the rest of the church was heavily restored in 1856 and during the early 20th century. This picture shows the church after its restoration. It was not until another ten years had elapsed before Littleover became a separate parish from Mickleover, Findern and Potlock.*

Interior of St Peter's Church. *This late 1800s picture shows the church after its restoration in 1856, when the North Aisle was rebuilt. In 1872 the north organ chamber and vestry were built, the chancel floor was tiled and choir stalls erected. The South Aisle was added in 1908. Traces of the old church still remain, the Norman doorway being the most conspicuous, which is now incorporated into the main body of the church as a result of an extension. The font is also a survivor from the old church. The plate and chalice date from 1687, the latter a gift from John Harpur.*

DCHQ503733 - Picture courtesy of A P Knighton

Church Street. *The row of cottages which line Church Street and back onto St Peter's churchyard are said to have cost £17 each when they were built. This was where the original village used to stand, which consisted of a number of tiny houses, clustered round the church, built using mud and stone or timber framing with thatched roofs. Farming was the main pre-occupation of the villagers. For centuries the area near the bottom of Shepherd Street, around where the White Swan now stands, was the centre for village gatherings. Here there was a square where fairs, feasts and markets were held and ceremonies would take place on public holidays.*

The Old Cottage, The Hollow. *The Old Cottage in the Hollow at Littleover, pictured in the 1880s is the oldest property in the village, and one of the few in Derby to retain its thatch. No one knows its precise age, but it probably started life as a labourers' cottage in the 16th century. The Page family lived there for several centuries and Walter Haynes, the village hedge-cutter, is also listed as an occupant. It operated as an inn for a time before reverting to a private residence. The inn did a particularly good trade when race meetings took place at nearby Hell Meadow. Following the threat of demolition it was restored between 1966 and 1975 and is now Grade II listed.*

DRBY002112 - Picture courtesy of Derby City Council

DRBY003710 - Picture courtesy of Derby City Council

Littleover Hollow. *In the 19th century, The Hollow at Littleover became a favourite haunt of artists, who would sit and paint the scene. Nowadays neither they nor the workman taking a rest on his wheelbarrow would be safe on what has become a very busy thoroughfare. The road above the cottage used to carry straight on and the sharp bend to the east was presumably introduced by the Heathcote family. They succeeded the Harpurs at The Old Hall, and no doubt changed the road alignment to benefit their own house and grounds. The bend, apart from causing motorists to slow, does add an extra touch of charm to the scene. This picture dates back to 1928.*

DRBY000220 - Picture courtesy of Derby Evening Telegraph

Derby High School for Girls, Hillsway. *When it was considered the school premises off Osmaston Road were unsuitable for further development, a new site was found for Derby High School for Girls. In 1956 work started on building the new school, on a three acre site at the junction of Burton Road and Hillsway. Originally it comprised of a six-bed roomed property known as Hilltop, a lodge, orchard, extensive lawns and flower beds. The school was designed to provide modern up to date facilities for 370 to 400 pupils. The existing access from Burton Road was closed and two new entrances off Hillsway were provided.*

Derbyshire Fire Service Headquarters, Burton Road. *The Old Hall was originally built as a Manor House by Sir Richard Harpur. It hides behind the attractive half-timbered Lodge House on Burton Road. The Harpurs held high office in Derbyshire, but the last of the line died in 1754, and the Old Hall passed to Samuel Heathcote. Later Thomas Heathcote revamped the property in the middle of the 18th century and it was rebuilt completely in the 1890s by its new owners, the McInnes family who remained in occupation until after the First World War. The house was then let for a time, before being sold to Rolls-Royce. It is now the headquarters of the Derbyshire Fire Service.*

DRBY000232 - Picture courtesy of Derby Evening Telegraph

DRBY007608 - Picture courtesy of Derby Evening Telegraph

Fire at The Grange, Burton Road. *The Grange stands behind the supermarket on Burton Road and, like nearby Littleover House, lost its park to the developers. A large white house, it was built in the early 1800s and at one time was occupied by Rueben Eastwood a local iron-founder. It was Eastwood who added the campanile so that he had somewhere to go after dinner to smoke. In the mornings the glow from his foundry, which he could see in the distance, ensured that his workers were hard at work. The Grange is now in the hands of the Freemasons and the stables have been converted into a community centre. Following the fire in April 1991, the hall has been substantially refurbished.*

The Pastures, Pastures Hill. *This picture shows the Mayor of Derby Abraham Woodiwiss at his home 'The Pastures' with members of the Council, Board of Guardians and School Board in 1881. The Pastures was built in 1785, for Josias Cockshutt and in 1880 it was acquired by Sir Abraham Woodiwiss. He was a self made man, who after working as a stonemason went into engineering, building many bridges including Trent Bridge at Nottingham. He also went into partnership with another Derby man, forming the company Benton and Woodiwiss, who laid many of the main railway lines in the country. He was responsible for building the Strand and the Strand Arcade, in Derby.*

DRBY007744 - Picture courtesy of Derby City Council

MICKLEOVER

The large residential suburb of Mickleover is located on the western outskirts of Derby. Most of the development there took place during the 20th century. But in an area close to the Uttoxeter Road are a number of interesting old buildings of such historical importance that in 1975 Conservation Area status was awarded. Mickleover was settled by the Saxons and probably by the Romans before then. The discovery of a large amount of Roman coins in 1988, when a school extension was being built, added weight to that theory. In addition, Rykneld Street, constructed by the Romans, ran though Littleover only a short distance away, on the other side of Mickleover Moor.

Prior to the Norman invasion, Mickleover was a royal manor, but William the Conqueror gave it, together with Littleover, Findern and Potlock, a now deserted medieval village, to the Abbots of Burton Abbey. Life was difficult under the Abbots with several serious disputes about taxes. Following the Dissolution of the Monasteries, the manor of Mickleover was granted to Sir William Paget, by Henry VIII, and over the next few centuries changed hands several times.

The rapid expansion of industrialisation in Derby during the 18th and 19th centuries led to over-crowding in the centre of the town. This resulted in the better off starting to look further afield to build their houses and Mickleover seemed ideal for their requirements.

Despite the rapid expansion of Mickleover in the 20th century, Derby did not absorb the village until 1968. This meant that, rather inconveniently for those who lived on the western side of the village, the Uttoxeter Trolley bus service and, for a short time, the motorbus service that took its place only ran as far as the Borough boundary. The boundary extension solved this problem and Corporation buses no longer stopped short of the village centre.

Trail: The Square – Etwall Road – Pastures (detour) – Mickleover Manor – Orchard Street – The Hollow – Uttoxeter Road – Station Road – Limes Avenue.

The Square, Mickleover (previously called the Market Place)

In the days when Mickleover was only a small village, the Market Place was used to stage the Annual Wakes on the first Monday following the 6 December. Plough Monday and the Harvest Festival were also celebrated in the village by the predominantly farming community. The Market Place was also a stopping place for horse drawn transport. In the 1800s, a coach passed through the village en route to Newcastle-under-Lyme, three days per week, returning on the following day. In 1932, the Market Place lost the elegant drinking fountain, which was replaced by a cast-iron switchbox to control the newly installed electric lighting.

DCHQ503714 - Picture courtesy of A P Knighton

DRBY007439 - Picture courtesy of Keene, Richard

All Saints Church, Etwall Road. *William the Conqueror is recorded as giving Mickleover, with its church, to Burton Abbey, but there is no mention of a church in the Domesday Book. The present church has early 14th century origins, which can be seen from the stonework in the tower, but mainly dates from 1858; this picture was taken shortly afterwards in 1862. At that time it underwent extensive restoration by H. I. Stevens. A clock with only two faces was installed by John Smith in 1895; with open fields to the north and east no more were required. Further works were carried out during the 20th century, including the provision of a Lady Chapel, consecrated in June 1967.*

Coffins in the crypt of All Saints Church, Etwall Road. *The crypt was discovered after Mr Baker, the verger at All Saints Church, fell five feet down into it, when the slab that was covering the entrance cracked and broke into two pieces. The gravestone which had been placed above it was dated 1712. It contained an ancient vault belonging to the Newton family. The Manor House next to the church was described as 'the ancient seat of the Newton family'. The Newtons had a history of holding public offices and members of the family were Mayors of Derby, Sheriffs of Derbyshire and Parliamentarians on numerous occasions. The picture was taken in 1989.*

DRBY007800 - Picture courtesy of Derby Evening Telegraph

Mickleover Manor (Woodlands). *The present house was built around the middle of the 19th century and replaced a much older property. For many years it was the home of the Newton family, before they moved to Lockington Hall, at the end of the First World War. Sir Frederick and Lady Inglefield lived there for several years, before it was let as a private preparatory school for boys aged from five to 14. The school closed in 1950, and the Local Authority took over the premises and turned them into the Woodland Hospital for the elderly. This closed in 1989 and the building has been converted into apartments. The picture dates from 1864.*

County Lunatic Asylum (Pastures Hospital). *This 1848 picture pre-dates the opening of the Derbyshire Pauper Lunatic Asylum in 1851, later known as Pastures Hospital. The original estate covered an area of 79 acres with 32 acres enclosed by a brick wall nearly a mile long. Patients came from Union Workhouses all over the county, many of them having been kept in atrocious conditions. Once freed of chains and restraints they found that not only were they given proper care and attention, but also that there were opportunities for recreation and relaxation amidst beautiful countryside. Many of the men worked on the hospital farm and the women attended to domestic jobs. The hospital closed in the late 20th century and the land is now taken up by housing.*

DCHQ501537 - Picture courtesy of A P Knighton

Old Hall, Orchard Street. *The Old Hall is thought to be the oldest building in the village. It was originally called The Cedars and is a delightful, well preserved timber-framed house of red bricks and black oak beams. It was built for William Cotchett, whose son Robert inherited it in 1635. Robert took the side of the Parliamentarians during the Civil War and because of his views he was banished for a time, before returning to his home in 1648. Some historians think this is the reason for the date carved above the door. According to legend Oliver Cromwell stayed at the house when his troops stormed Tutbury Castle.*

The Hollow. *This picture of cottages in The Hollow was taken in 1912. Particularly of note is The Old Hollow Cottage, which dates from the 17th century. It is a fine old timber-framed cottage that once had a thatched-roof. A horse trough has been placed near the bottom of the hill, which was once used by both horses and humans, when The Hollow was a through road. Brookfield School was built at the bottom of The Hollow after the road had been closed to through traffic in the late 20th century.*

DRBY001864 - Picture courtesy of Derby City Council

Mickleover Board School, Uttoxeter Road. *Mickleover Board School for boys and girls was erected on the Uttoxeter Road in 1880 and significantly expanded in 1907. It accommodated 250 pupils of all ages and adequately met the educational requirements of all the children in the village. Since then the population of Mickleover has increased enormously and the children are accommodated in a number of schools around the area. The Old School has been converted into a successful Community Centre and has received several awards as the best in Derby. There is an excellent tearoom, staffed by volunteers, that serves morning coffee and light lunches for both local people and visitors alike.*

Old Mickleover Board School, Uttoxeter Road. *An unusual event occurred at the school on Wednesday 7 February 1900, when the first children's matinee in a British cinema took place on the premises. The matinee preceded a film for adults. Exactly why the show took place at Mickleover, which never had a cinema, is not known and there is no record of any further shows being held. In fact, it was more than ten years later before Derby had its first purpose-built cinema and sometime after that before regular children's matinees were introduced.*

DCHQ503715 - Picture courtesy of A P Knighton

Station Road. *The arrival in the late 1870s of the railway in Mickleover, with its station over one mile from the centre of the village, led to a housing expansion in that direction. Two quiet country roads, Goosecroft Road and Mackworth Road, were renamed Station Road. It only took six minutes to get to Friargate Station (GNR always used one word), in the centre of Derby and the same time to return, which attracted many new residents, who liked the idea of living in the country. The brickyard opposite the station was enlarged and a number of large villas and smaller houses were built along the tree-lined road.*

Mickleover for Radburn Railway Station (the name Great Northern Railway gave to the station). *The Great Northern Railway built the station, on their Ilkeston to Egginton line, in the late 1870s. It was about one mile from the centre of the village, in a cutting off Mackworth Road, now Station Road. The main purpose of the line was to carry freight, with a limited passenger service also available. The service did not have a particularly long life, closing for regular passenger trains in 1939 along with Egginton Junction and Etwall Station, following the withdrawal of LNER services to Burton-upon-Trent. Excursion trains continued to call for a number of years, before total closure on 3 February 1964. However, the line itself remained open for a further four years for testing purposes. The Great Northern Inn provides a nostalgic reminder of the line.*

DRBY000153 - Picture courtesy of Derby City Council

Mickleover Windmill, Off Station Road. *The building of the Derby Pauper Lunatic Asylum in 1851, led to the moving of the windmill which had previously stood on land at Field Mill Farm. It was rebuilt on Mickleover Common, on a site just off Station Road, pictured in 1969. The windmill was demolished and the land covered by a housing development in the 1970s. Another windmill stood on the west side of Chain Lane, Littleover at its junction with Burton Road. Chain Lane got its unusual name because it had a chain stretched across the road to stop carriages using it to avoid paying a toll.*

DCHQ000814 - Picture courtesy of Brighouse Collection

The Limes, Limes Avenue. *The Limes was built around 1836, for Samuel Wright, a wealthy local business man, who was a silk throwster. It was, and still is, a handsome mansion with a lovely conservatory and good field views. It is now a residential home. The old brick cottages which used to flank the narrow entrance to Limes Avenue, apart from one restored cottage have been demolished. Along Uttoxeter Road at the top of Limes Avenue, a parade of modern shops has been built with a Tesco Supermarket at the rear.*

DRBY002373 - Picture courtesy of Derby Evening Telegraph

CHAPTER 14 - NORMANTON, ROSEHILL AND PEARTREE

Normanton grew from an ancient rural village, originally named Normanton-by-Derby, which is thought to have been the site of one of the major Viking settlements in the Derby area. It was sited, in present day terms to the south of the Ring Road around Village Street, close to St Giles Church. However, the industrialisation of Derby saw the picture change and the farmland started to be used for housing. This gave birth to New Normanton, although the whole area covered by the former village and the new development is nowadays usually just referred to as Normanton. Nevertheless, it is still correct to refer to the older settlement as Normanton-by-Derby.

By 1928 Normanton had become part of the Borough of Derby, which at the time needed to build new dwellings to re-house people living in condemned houses in Derby. The initial part of the Derby Arterial Road on the south side of the town was built with municipal housing estates on either side. Normanton Park, referred to by locals as 'Normanton Rec', was created at the bottom of Warwick Avenue, where it joined Stenson Road and led to the Cavendish, named after the Duke of Devonshire's family.

Normanton Barracks, latterly the headquarters of the Sherwood Foresters regiment was once a prominent local landmark, until it was demolished in 1981. There was some initial apprehension in Normanton about the military setting up their Head Quarters in the village. That soon disappeared and turned to a feeling of great respect for the officers and men who lived at the barracks. Church parade on Sunday mornings was a very colourful affair, as the soldiers marched to St Giles Church, led by the band and regimental mascot, the ram - known as Private Derby. The men always sat in the south aisle, which became known as the 'soldier aisle'. For many years the regimental colours were displayed in the church, but they are now on display in the regimental museum at Nottingham Castle.

The Arboretum was opened on the 16 September 1840 and became England's first public park. It was Joseph Strutt, the third son of the great industrialist Jedidiah, who donated the Arboretum to the people of Derby. He commissioned John Claudius Loudon, a renowned writer and garden designer, to draw up the plans. Loudon laid the park out with mounds planted with trees and shrubs to disguise the paths and park boundaries to give the illusion of space. No two species of tree or shrub were the same in the 11 acre park

Trail: Normanton – Rosehill – Peartree – Arboretum.

Looking east down Village Street, before the road was widened. *Village Street was part of an ancient trackway, which probably led from the River Derwent. In the 1880s, when this picture was taken, Normanton was an attractive place to visit with its tall elms and chestnut trees. Many of the gardens in the village had large orchards and although at the time of this picture, the village was getting busier, there is not a vehicle of any description to be seen on the road. However, only a short distance away the Cavendish was beginning to take shape as a busy shopping centre and houses were much in demand. Mr Brownsword the verger and his wife can be seen in the picture. The trees on the left are near where the Greyhound Public House now stands.*

DRBY000750 - Picture courtesy of Derby City Council

DRBY007869 - Picture courtesy of Derby City Council

Normanton House, Village Street. *Pictured c1900 is Normanton House, which was built in the 1740s for the Dixies. In the 1800s the attractively laid out grounds were often used for local fund raising events. After changing hands several times, it was purchased in 1906 by Giles Austin, who was the owner of a high class grocery business in Derby, and after whom the Austin Estate was named. He built himself a new house in the grounds, Homelands House, and rented out Normanton House. During World War II it was occupied by the Army and after the war it was used as a Course Centre for the National Nursery Examination Board. It later became part of Homelands School, operating as a sixth form block.*

Normanton Infants School, Browning Street - Centenary Celebrations. *On the 26 April 1880, Normanton Board School was opened by the headmaster William Powell, admitting 16 boys and 21 girls. Miss Elizabeth Duddell was the infants sewing mistress. A change in the law in 1902 abolished School Boards and replaced them with Local Education Authority Schools run by Councils. By this time the number of children and staff had increased and in 1925 all seven classes had 60 or over on their registers. Shortly afterwards it was decided to build an extension, but the Ministry of Education would not agree to it forming part of the existing school, which led to the creation of Normanton Infant School.*

DRBY002501 - Picture courtesy of Derby Evening Telegraph

DRBY006581 - Picture courtesy of Derby City Council

The Old Church of St Giles, Village Street. The earliest written mention of the church was in 1288, in documents relating to a dispute between the abbot of Darley Abbey and the parishioners over repairs and maintenance to the building. However, there has been a church on the site for much longer, which might even pre-date the Normans. In 1861, the old church was demolished and replaced by the present building by Giles and Brookhouse of Derby, with only the Norman tympanum and tower surviving. Further extensions were carried out in 1893 and at the beginning of the 20th century. This is a c1850 drawing and internal plan of the church.

DRBY003274 - Picture courtesy of Derby Evening Telegraph

Font at St Giles' Church, 1981.

Interior of St Giles' Church, 1981.

DRBY007618 - Picture courtesy of Derby Evening Telegraph

NCCN001302 - Picture courtesy of Derby City Council

Sherwood Foresters Foreign Service Company at Normanton Barracks, Derby, 1900. *Sherwood Foresters before leaving for the Boer War at an unknown location (the picture was donated to Retford Library. W W Winter, the photographer was based in Derby) A web site user has identified this picture and gave 'Picture the Past' the following information:- 'This picture is of the Volunteer Company prior to leaving the Depot at Normanton Barracks, Derby for foreign service in South Africa. The 1st Volunteer Company was formed on the 24th February 1900, and was taken on strength of the 1st Btn 10th April it was 115 strong and its Officers were Capt Turner Lee, 1st Notts, Lieut R.K.Ellis, 4th Notts Militia,Lieut F.A.C.Wright, 1st Derbyshire Volunteers. Pte 7353 Joseph Wingfield lived with his Father and Sister at The Gutter, off Nottingham Road, Belper. 7376 Cpl Oscar Taylor was formerly a Mining Engineer & came from Chesterfield, 7357 Pte R.A.Tinker from Derby later served in the Territorials and died in the 1950's. Sgt Blackwall came from an Army family in the Wirksworth area.' There is a long list of the names of soldiers present. Starting at the rear left :- Gregory, Lacey, Brown, Hickman, Swindell, Kelham, Blackney, Gamble, Jacks, Jackson, Crofts, MacMilan, Martin, Skevington, Herod, Hickinbottom. 2nd Row:- Ormesher, Farnesworth, Newbold, Wingfield, Walker, Cotterill, Clews, Dyson, Tattersall, Cooper, Edge, Champion, Moisey, Lane, Chatterton, Phillips, Smith, Forman, Wheewall, Austin, Soar, Goodlad, Johnson, Green. 3rd Row:- Piggford, Leek, Castleton, A Taylor W Taylor, Cotteril, Turner, Braddock, Frith, Hargreave, Atkin, Russell Warburton, Welbourne, Mason, White, Littlewood, McLeod, Jones, Stanley, Pick, Hardy, Gurnhill, Chappell, Sgt. Inst. Lattimore, Henson, E White, Brailsford, Fk. White Goodlad, Depledge, T Holmes, Norton, J Holmes, Peake, Walpole, Naylor, Bancroft, Laker, Poynter, Jones, Baker, Holland, Smith, Parker, Tinker, Simpson, Mills, Angliss, Hickinbottom. Front Row:- Cox, Millward, Manifold, Moreton, Bunting, Asman, Ward, Corporal Wild, Corporal Widnall, Sgt Mackenzie, Sgt Marshall, Colour Sgt Deniham. Lieutenant Kingdon Ellis. Capt Turner Lee, Lieutenant Cedric Wright, Sgt Blackwall, Corporal Essex, Sgt Austin, Corporal Taylor, Webourne, Heanes, Kirk, Taylor, Johnson, Malkin, P?*

Land Defence Volunteers, Normanton Barracks. *The barracks were opened on 1st December 1877 as the headquarters for the 54th and 95th regiments who later became the Sherwood Foresters. During the Boer War and First World War it was an important training and deployment depot. It became very much a part of village life in Normanton, before the Sherwood Foresters eventually left in 1963. The site was cleared in 1982 and although the new development was named the Forester Leisure Park as a reminder of its past, nothing remains of its distinguished history. The picture was taken in 1915.*

DRBY004708 - Picture courtesy of Derby City Council

DRBY007734 - Picture courtesy of Derby City Council

Elderly former Sherwood Foresters, at Normanton Barracks. *Pictured in 1938 are a group of former Sherwood Foresters who survived the Sikkim Campaign. The Sikkim Gun is pictured in the foreground. The 2nd Battalion took part in the Sikkim Expedition to Tibet in 1888, when the gun was captured at Rinchingong and presented to the Derbyshire Regiment by Lord Curzon, then Viceroy of India. In the centre is Major-General Sir Frederick Maurice KCMG CB, Colonel of the Sherwood Foresters.*

Territorial Army march past Normanton Barracks. *Following the demolition of Normanton Barracks, shortly after this picture was taken in 1980, the site was redeveloped and renamed the Foresters Leisure Park. The Showcase cinema complex occupies a substantial part of the new development. There is also a bowling alley, bingo hall, hotel and a pub. The pub is most unusual in design, as it is styled in the form of a traditional oast house, common in the south east of the country, but not in Derbyshire. The Oast House pub has recently been refurbished and the interior now no longer attempts to relate to the appearance of the exterior. The soldiers are walking past the former cookhouse wall, down Sinfin Lane.*

DRBY000668 - Picture courtesy of Derby Evening Telegraph

DRBY000680 - Picture courtesy of Derby Evening Telegraph

Napoleon's Willow, Normanton Barracks. *A plaque, which marked this famous tree when it stood close to the sports field at Normanton Barracks, is now held by Derby Museum. The words on the plaque are as follows: 'THE NAPOLEON WILLOW From the tree, now dead, which grew over the tomb of Napoleon 1st at St. Helena, a slip was brought by Sir Reginald Hart, V.C. and planted near Rugby in 1909. From this Sir Reginald's son, Colonel R.S. Hart, D.S.O, of our Regiment, took another slip and planted it here in 1931.' The picture was taken in November 1980. A large willow tree was grown at the Territorial Army Centre in Sinfin Lane from a cutting taken from the barracks. For a short time after the de-commissioning of the barracks some buildings were let as industrial/commercial units. Several car repair businesses were housed at the site.*

Cavendish Cross Roads. *The Cavendish Hotel, when it was built in 1898, gave its name to the area, where five roads met; Stenson Road, Almond Street, Upper Dale Road, Walbrook Road and Derby Lane. In 1910, the sizeable Derby Co-operative Provident Society was built, which helped to establish a thriving shopping area. The other shops in the area looked rather small in comparison, but helped to provide a wide range of facilities. Birds Bakery stood at the junction of Upper Dale Road and Almond Street, by the box where the tram conductors clocked in and out on the route to and from Derby. For a number of years the Bird family used to park their cars outside the bakery, which included an E Type Jaguar and a Jensen Interceptor. A tram can be seen in the picture approaching the Cavendish Hotel. The picture was taken c1910.*

Co-operative Provident Society Ltd., Stenson Road. *In 1910, the Derby Cooperative Provident Society opened a store at the point where Stenson Road is joined by Almond Street at the Cavendish. Here a two storeyed building was erected on a semi-circular frontage, with shops for grocery, butchery and a creamery. It used to have cash carriers that went through holes in the walls between departments to take your cash and return with change. The building was of an elaborate design, in brick with stone facings. According to Leslie Unsworth in his book 'Seventy-Five Years of Co-operation in Derby' it was 'the most imposing block of buildings the Society has ever erected'. The first floor of the building was occupied by the Jubilee Hall, which seated over 400 people. The arcade, 'monkey run' at the front of building was a popular meeting place for young people. The picture is c1948.*

DRBY001567 - Picture courtesy of Derby City Council

Derby Pavilion, Derby Lane. *In 1902, a local farmer agreed to the erection of a marquee on his land at the junction of Stenson Road and Derby Lane, which at first was used for auctions and local talent competitions. Later, it was awarded a music licence and this led to touring concert parties and repertory companies performing at the venue. It was replaced by a wooden building, which accommodated over 600 people, the 'chicken run' at the rear of the hall provided standing room for children. It became known as the Derby Pierrot Pavilion, but was burnt down in 1929 and only replaced eight years later by the Cavendish Cinema. On a Saturday morning the Cavendish Cinema had a matinee for children, which was very popular. Staff used to put a rope across Stenson Road at finishing time to form a temporary crossing point for the hundreds of children. The site is now taken up by a supermarket. Picture is c1920.*

Normanton Recreation Ground. *Normanton Rec as it is still frequently called, pictured c1910, is now known officially as Normanton Park. It was developed on the site of old brickyards and opened in 1909, to provide a place where local people could relax and enjoy fresh air, in a heavily populated area. The park linked 'Old Normanton' with the newer and rapidly expanding industrial, inner-urban Normanton. Part of its southern boundary was lost to Warwick Avenue when the Ring Road was built, but tree planting helped to soften the gap that had been created. The trees are now well established and there are wide pathways round the park. On the Warwick Avenue side of the park a car park has been provided and there are also foot entrances from Chatsworth Street and Fairfield Road. Following repeated vandalism the park has been substantially refurbished.*

DRBY003313 - Picture courtesy of Derby City Council

DRBY007508 - Picture courtesy of Derby City Council

View from Walbrook Road up St Thomas's Road. *This c1920 picture looking up St Thomas's Road from the junction with Walbrook Road shows the road to be quiet, with only pedestrians and one parked car to be seen. Walbrook Road is one of the five roads that radiate from the Cavendish. It is an ancient thoroughfare and appears on the 1605 map of Normanton. Electric trams started running along Walbrook Road and St Thomas's Road from 8 September 1905 and the Cavendish became an important shopping area. The rails were covered over after the trams had stopped running on the 17 March 1934, and the wiring was then used by trolleybuses.*

Auxiliary Fire Service 'Firewatch' Demonstration, Haddon Street. *The picture shows the Auxiliary Fire Service in action in 1941. The service was created by an Act of Parliament shortly before the outbreak of the Second World War, when AFS members worked alongside the regular fireman. During the Blitz in Derby - June 25, 1940, to July 9, 1941 - 28 civilians were killed in their homes, workplaces and in the streets of the town. Another 22 died in the Rolls-Royce raid in July, 1942. After that only one other person died as a result of a raid. That was Henry John Norman Rowe (47) who was injured on June 15, 1944, at Ashbourne Airfield and died the same day in Derbyshire Royal Infirmary.*

DRBY001213 - Picture courtesy of Derby Evening Telegraph

The Mafeking Hotel, Porter Road. *The Mafeking Hotel pictured in 1938 was opened at the turn of the century as the Bowling Green Inn. The name was changed to commemorate the lifting of the siege of Mafeking. This achievement was the most celebrated act of the Second Boer War, when Colonel Robert Baden-Powell and a detachment of British troops and townspeople were besieged by the Dutch-Afrikaner Boers. The Boers surrounded the town for 217 days, before relief arrived on the 17 May 1900. News of the liberation of the town was greeted with great jubilation in this country, the celebrations being known as 'mafficking'. The pub is now closed and the bowling green, which caused considerable embarrassment to many visiting bowlers who failed to fully take into account the steep fall, scheduled for redevelopment.*

Horse and Tram outside Normanton Hotel, Normanton Road. *This 1901 picture shows a double deck horse drawn tram standing proudly outside the Normanton Hotel. It was replaced a few years later by Derby Corporation electric trams. The first electric tram operated from the Cavendish on the 8 September 1904. A year later the tram route was extended round the corner to the left and along Walbrook Road, St Thomas's Road, Dairy House Road and Douglas Street to join the Osmaston Road and London Road routes. This created a circular route via the Cavendish, on which trams continued to operate until replaced by trolleybuses in 1934.*

DRBY001403 - Picture courtesy of C Beech

300th Anniversary Procession of Sikh Nation Celebrations, Upper Dale Road DRBY001403 Courtesy C. Beech

Normanton is home to a high ethnic minority population, where the largest concentrations of Derby's Asian community live. In particular, Normanton Road, the very busy main thoroughfare, which leads to the centre of Derby, has numerous Asian shops, businesses and fast food outlets and is well known for its range of Indian, Pakistani and Bangladeshi restaurants. In addition, the expansion of the European Union in 2004 has brought new immigrants to the area from various Eastern European countries. There are a wide number of places of worship in the Normanton area, which serve different religions. The streets are frequently colourfully decorated for religious festivals as in the picture above taken on the 18 April 1999, when the Sikh's celebrated their 300th anniversary.

DRBY000813 - Picture courtesy of Derby City Council

Pear Tree bridge and railway. *An early 20th century picture of Pear Tree bridge and railway station platform. Opened on the 2 June 1890, Pear Tree and Normanton Railway Station had a dispute as to who was the first passenger to board the train. The first train of the day to Derby stopped there at 7.41am and was no doubt primarily used by people going to work. The booking office is at the top of the embankment fronting onto Osmaston Park Road, which runs across the bridge over the line. Gas lamps were used to light the platforms. The redeveloped area was named after Pear Tree Farm, which once stood on the site.*

Sir Frederick Roberts Public House, Pear Tree Road - Charabanc Outing. *Charabanc outings were very popular after the First World War. Here a party of men are having their photograph taken in 1922, prior to departure. The children in the picture have probably been brought along to see their fathers off. It is interesting to note that nearly all the men are dressed very smartly and appear to be wearing ties and some form of headgear. The Sir Frederick Roberts public house was on Pear Tree Road; it was converted from a corner shop in the late 1800s and survived until 1997 before being demolished. It was known to the locals as 'Dicky Birds' after the first landlord who was something of a local character.*

DRBY000386 - Picture courtesy of Derby City Council

DRBY007730 - Picture courtesy of Derby City Council

The Mayor of Derby, Sir Thomas Roe, receiving guests at Derby Arboretum. *Joseph Strutt, the third son of the great industrialist Jedidiah, donated the Arboretum to the people of Derby. He commissioned John Claudius Loudon, a renowned writer and garden designer, to draw up the plans. Loudon laid the park out with mounds planted with trees and shrubs to disguise the paths, and park boundaries to give the illusion of space. No two species of tree or shrub were the same in the 11 acre park, which was opened on the 16 September 1840, and became England's first public park. In this picture Sir Thomas Roe, who served three terms as Mayor of Derby, is seen welcoming guests to what is thought to be part of Queen Victoria's Diamond Jubilee celebrations in 1897.*

Derby Arboretum in the snow. *Joseph Strutt was a great social reformer and recognised the fact that the working classes, though better off regarding housing and working conditions, were being deprived of open space. He wanted the people to have a 'Pleasure Ground or Recreation Ground to offer the inhabitants of the town the opportunity of enjoying, together with their families, exercise and recreation in the fresh air, in public walks and grounds devoted to that purpose.' This was achieved and when the task had been completed by John Claudius Loudon, he named the park, 'The Arboretum', pictured here c1904. To encourage an appreciation of art, Strutt opened up his home, Thorntree House in Derby, when requested to do so on Sundays. This enabled visitors to view his interesting collection of paintings.*

DRBY005325 - Picture courtesy of Derby City Council

DRBY005330 - Picture courtesy of Derby City Council

The 'Florentine Boar' statue in Derby Arboretum. *The Florentine Boar was a hollow earthenware copy made by William John Coffee from 19th century drawings of an original bronze fountain, which sits on the edge of the Marketo Nuovo in Florence. Coffee's copy of the boar became a popular attraction at the Arboretum. Seen here c1904, it was refurbished in 1934, but damaged by a bomb during the Second World War and removed. Following years of decline, funding was obtained from the Heritage Lottery, the Council and other sources, and the Arboretum, together with the boar, were restored to their former glory early in 2007.*

DRBY006698 - Picture courtesy of Derby City Council

East Lodge, showing the public room, 1840.

Arboretum Entrance, c1910.

DMAG000114 - Picture courtesy of Derby Museums and Art Gallery